# THE PSALMS:
## The Prayer Book of Jesus

J.W. Gregg Meister

# THE PSALMS: THE PRAYER BOOK OF JESUS

iUniverse books may be ordered through booksellers or by contacting:

iUniverse
1663 Liberty Drive
Bloomington, IN 47403
www.iuniverse.com
1-800-Authors (1-800-288-4677)

Because of the dynamic nature of the internet, any web addresses or links contained in
this book may have changed since publication and may no longer be valid. The views
expressed in this work are solely those of the author and do not necessarily reflect the
views of the publisher, and the publisher hereby disclaims any responsibility for them.

Scripture taken from the Holy Bible, New International Version® NIV®
Copyright © 1973, 1978,1984 by International Bible Society.
Used by permission of Zondervan Publishing House. °All rights reserved worldwide.

ISBN: 978-1-5320-7220-8 (sc)
ISBN: 978-1-5320-7221-5 (e)

Library of Congress Control Number: 2019903560

Print information available on the last page.

iUniverse rev. date: 03/29/2019

To

My Mother

She taught us that our speech should always be gracious.
But seasoned with salt (Colossians 4:6).

# Contents

Acknowledgements.............................................................................. ix

An Invitation...................................................................................... 1
Your Battlefield Promise, Psalm 1....................................................... 5
From Despair to Exaltation, Psalm 22...............................................11
Your Best Protection, Psalm 23 .........................................................17
The Best Experience Yet, Psalm 34.................................................... 27
The Peaceable Kingdom, Psalm 37 .................................................... 33
Seeking Good News, Psalm 46 ........................................................... 41
In God We Trust, Psalm 56 ................................................................ 47
Your Surprise Ending, Psalm 90........................................................ 55
It's All in the Family, Psalm 103........................................................ 63
Stepping Along, Psalms 120 to 134 ................................................... 71
Search and Destroy! Psalm 139 ......................................................... 77
Between the Pasture and the Palace, Psalm 142 ................................. 87
Deeper Disciples, Psalm 143 ............................................................. 95

Endnotes...........................................................................................101
Discussion Questions .......................................................................103
Selected Psalms: 1, 22, 23, 34, 37, 46, 56, 90, 103, 120-121:2,
139, 142, 143 ................................................................................ 109

# Acknowledgements

Production is a team sport. That's been my mantra since I started Interlink Media in 1988, and it applies equally well to writing this book on the psalms. I'm grateful beyond measure to Lakeside Presbyterian Church in San Francisco when that church took a leap of faith and called a 30-year-old to be their pastor. That congregation allowed me, for 11 years, to explore the Book of Psalms for my personal growth and as a resource for pastoral care and preaching. A quarter of a century later my colleague, Rev. Bill Gaskill, pastor of First Presbyterian Church in Merchantville, New Jersey, asked me to fill that pulpit for six weeks while he was on sabbatical. Around this time Christ Presbyterian Church in Gibbstown, New Jersey, invited me to be their guest preacher on several occasions. Pastor Anthony Talton and the congregation at Mt. Olivet Baptist Church in Haddonfield, New Jersey, have welcomed me into their fellowship and granted me the privilege of preaching and leading in Bible study. Those parish experiences form the basis for these chapters.

Dr. Ken Culver, Rev. Cindy Alloway, and Mr. Jeff Spragens, founders of Foundation for Peace, hired me for over a decade to produce fundraising and volunteer recruitment videos. This allowed me to live among some of the most impoverished men, women, and children in our hemisphere. Participating in work and worship with these people as they praise the Lord for all His goodness to them is a humbling experience.

This book would still be in its intermediate writing stages were it not for my Williams College classmate, Peter Hassinger, who awakened me from my writing slumber and launched me on a writing schedule. As friend, mentor, and editor, Peter would be the first to say that he bears absolutely no responsibility for the ideas expressed herein, but he would admit to providing several of the critical writing strategies that produced them. Graphic artist Chris Prasol and I have worked together since my first television productions in the 1990s as he refined and created my visuals with his graphic skills. Fortunately, he responded positively to my request for help with the design work in the print medium. Skilled hobbyist Edward H. Draper gave me his inlaid woodcut of Jesus at prayer in 1970. It's been on my office wall since then, and now graces the cover of this book. High school classmate and retired military chaplain Steve Doan pressed me to continue preaching after my stroke. Had he not done so, this book would not exist. My friend since seminary, John Mulder, suggested that I include discussion questions to facilitate adult education classes. Peter Horn, education consultant, brought his doctoral-level insights to the creation of that material. My Baptist friends, Mary and Jim McLaughlin, offered helpful comments on an early draft. Bruce and Deb Macleod have long indicated their interest in my finally writing this book, subtly strengthening my intentions to do so. Gordon Schaeffer's unique wisdom, generously offered on a consistent basis, is a special blessing. I appreciate the many people at iUniverse who are taking my words and transforming them into print and eBooks.

Perhaps I would have found my way to the psalms without my family, but that seems unlikely. My sister, Gretchen, and brother, Peter, have always been supportive of my spiritual journey in all its stages. My father's commitment to the ecclesiastical Body of Christ has sustained me even when we both saw its many shortcomings. His discipline in sermon preparation has been my model and is a testimony to his commitment to Jesus Christ. My daughter, Miriam Lucia, teaches me and inspires me and is part of my prayer life in the psalms more than she could ever know. My wife, Gail, has been my best friend since our marriage in 1971, my most ardent supporter, and my most skilled editor. We discovered Israel together. Understanding her Jewish roots has kept me from facile interpretations of what her tradition calls the Tanakh and what my tradition calls the Old Testament. I can attest that a good wife is "far more precious than jewels" (Proverbs 31:10).

None of us would be here were it not for our mothers. My mother taught me to love the psalms, to pray the psalms, and to memorize the psalms. Even more importantly, my mother taught me to love Jesus, for which I am eternally thankful.

J.W. Gregg Meister
New Jersey
2019

# An Invitation

"How do you know that the psalms were the prayer book of Jesus?" my friend asked me. "Because Jesus prayed them, and because as the Risen Christ He told us to look for Him in the psalms," I replied.

To elaborate, let's start by seeing how Jesus' prayer life defined Him and how the psalms permeated His prayer life.

- Jesus opened His ministry with 40 days of prayer and fasting in the wilderness.
- Jesus prefaced His decision as to which men He should call to become His disciples by spending the preceding night in prayer.
- Jesus regularly spent time alone in prayer, and these times invariably led to miraculous moments—feeding of the 5,000 (Matthew 14:13-21) and calming the storms on the Sea of Galilee, for example (Matthew 14:23-25).
- Jesus identified Himself with a central motif of the psalms when He said, "I am the Good Shepherd" (John 10:11), a clear reference to Psalm 23 that begins, "The Lord is my shepherd."
- Jesus credited His most challenging miracles of healing to the power of prayer. For example, He said, "This kind can be driven out only by prayer" (Mark 9:29), implying that His disciples were not practicing prayer sufficiently at that point.
- His disciples pointedly did not ask Christ to teach them how to raise money or run a political campaign or pull off a miracle. They asked Him how to pray. In response, He taught them the Lord's Prayer, which has distinct echoes from the psalms.

Most significantly, Jesus rehearsed the psalms on His deathbed, the cross. Bystanders reported overhearing him utter two direct quotes from the psalms, which form part of what we call the Seven Last Words: "My God, my God, why have you forsaken me?" (Matthew 27:46; Psalm 22:1) and "Father, into your hands I commend my spirit" (Luke 23:46; Psalm 31:5). And when Jesus moans, "I thirst," the Gospel of John (John 19:28) suggests that this is the fulfillment of Psalm 69:21 (with possible references also to Psalm 22:15, Psalm 42:2, and Psalm 63:1). It's as if our Lord is adding His signature to the Book of Psalms, showing us the psalms are essential and indispensable to His prayer life.

If these were the only references to the psalms from the lips of Jesus, that would be reason enough to study them.

For me, the title of this book comes not from His wounded lips but from His resurrected, healed lips. Sometime between Easter night and Pentecost 50 days later, the Risen Christ held a farewell meeting with His disciples. He explained to them, as they were still struggling to comprehend the meaning of His lovely life, ugly death, and triumphant reappearance, that "everything written about Me in the Law of Moses and the prophets *and the psalms* must be fulfilled" (Luke 24:44).

"Please read the psalms!" is the way I hear that explanation. Or better yet, "Please read, study, sing, and pray the psalms!" This, of course, does assuredly *not* mean that we are to ignore the Law of Moses (the first five books of the Bible) or the prophets with their strident warnings against ubiquitous idolatry and their equally vehement insistence upon social justice. We can discern the hidden Christ and the justice of Jesus permeating those texts.

But we especially meet our praying Prince of Peace in the Book of Psalms. From childhood, the psalms provided Him with comfort, support, and direction. If you want to know more about Jesus—if you want to know Jesus—then you are invited to read, study, sing, and pray the psalms.

I have been looking and I continue to look for Christ in the psalms. May you and I benefit in the same way those first disciples did when "He opened their minds to understand the scriptures" (Luke 24:45).

# Your Battlefield Promise

"The Lord watches over the way of the righteous" (Psalm 1:6).

We are in a battle. The Bible tells us so. In Genesis, tricked by the "serpent," the symbol of evil, we are kicked out of the Garden of Eden. Before the next ten verses are written, there's a murder. Violence and apocalyptic explosions rock the Book of Revelation, which closes the New Testament. Between these first and last books, the Bible looks like a photo gallery of battlefields, filled with images of death and disaster.

The Book of Psalms portrays this drama in remarkable detail. This is no surprise, for it reflects the personality of King David, who is credited with writing many of the psalms.

When you read the account of David's life, unadorned by the kinds of fantastical images we find in Greek mythology or Hollywood movies, you realize that David is one of history's most remarkable and influential men.

He's also one of the most violent.

From David's initial appearance in the biblical record to his dying breath, violence is part of David's life. We first meet him as a teenage shepherd, alone in the wilderness, protecting his sheep. Assuring King Saul that he is capable of fighting Goliath, David vividly describes the dangers a shepherd encounters. "I've killed bears, I've killed lions, to protect my sheep," David says. He's not reciting fables; he's reporting facts. He's not pretending he can kill; he's predicting what will happen to Goliath. He's not boasting about his own strength; he's believing in God's power (1 Samuel 17).

David slaughtered thousands and subdued kingdoms while establishing Israel and conquering Jerusalem—the paramount city in Biblical history and messianic prophecy, and still significant in world politics. Throughout his life, David was many things, sometimes simultaneously: a day laborer, a refugee, a king, an administrator, a musician, a poet and prophet, a father, a husband, a sinner, a saint. But from beginning to end, David was a warrior.

The historical books of the Bible record his exploits. The Book of Psalms records his inner life.[1]

David—and Jesus—considered the psalms, with their often-violent metaphors, as inspired by God. Jesus wraps His ministry around the psalms because Jesus knew that we are in a battle. Yes, we can and should think of the battle in familiar theological terms of the "flesh" versus the "spirit," of sin versus evil, of our earth-bound desires versus our eternal rewards.

But Jesus did not "spiritualize" this warfare. He knew its tragic human toll first hand. Jesus also knew the battle was waged on the terrain of power politics. Surely Mary, His mother, had told Him the part of the Christmas story we never read on Christmas Eve: How, during the family's escape to Egypt when Jesus was still a baby, King Herod killed all the baby boys in Bethlehem under the age of two (Matthew 2:16). King Herod had been told that a "king of the Jews" had recently been born. To protect his power and ward off another political insurrection—less than a decade earlier, the Jews had mounted a serious rebellion against the Roman Empire—Herod's government slaughtered the innocent in a bloody search for this baby king. The Gospel writer Matthew records that this mortal danger forced the baby Jesus and His parents to become refugees (Matthew 2:13). Several decades later when Jesus began his ministry, His cousin, John the Baptist, was imprisoned and ultimately beheaded in a brutal, public, political assassination. Jesus always knew He was on a battlefield.

The psalms were His battlefield companion—His prayer book. Jesus quoted and identified with them repeatedly and they permeate the New Testament. "The Lord is my shepherd" in the familiar Psalm 23 becomes "I am the Good Shepherd" in the Gospel of John (John 10:11). The first word of Psalm 1 ("blessed") became the key phrase in Jesus' Sermon on the Mount ("Blessed are those who…" Matthew 5:3-11). Jesus described His offer of salvation with concepts summarized in Psalm 103. When Jesus walked to Jerusalem for Passover, He prayed the Psalms of Ascents, a collection of psalms (Psalms 120-134) that can be read as a prayer book within the Book of Psalms. Jesus also suffered while praying the psalms, dying with them on His lips—with Psalm 22:1 recounted in Mark 15:34 and Psalm 31:5 recounted in Luke 23:46. As the Risen Christ, He directs us to the psalms when He says, "Everything must be fulfilled that is written about me in the Law of Moses, the prophets, *and the psalms*" (Luke 24:44).

We read, study, sing, and pray the psalms today not just because they were so important to Jesus, but also because we're in a battle. We face battles in our own culture and in our personal lives. There is no need to list them. We know we have personal struggles or we likely wouldn't attend church or have any interest in either Jesus or the psalms. There is also no need to recite the wicked and even satanic behaviors that are being propagated throughout our world.

What is important for us to know is that God has not abandoned us on the battlefields of life. We are not alone in the trenches of individual, cultural, or international warfare. The Risen Christ has directed us to His very own warrior's prayer book so that the psalms might become our field manual. The psalms can provide courage and conviction to guide us in our current conflict on behalf of the Gospel.

Psalm 1, with its very first word in verse 1, "blessed," launches us onto the battlefield.

Blessed? That's a battle cry? That's about as far from "Kill the infidel!" or even "Make America Great Again!" as one can imagine.

Here's one way to understand "blessed" as a battle cry. In the Hebrew, the original language of the Old Testament, the word for "blessed" is often translated as "happy" or "praiseworthy." We might read the first verse of this psalm as "Happy is the man or woman who does not walk in the counsel of the wicked" or "The person who does not live by the principles of the wicked is praiseworthy." In this instance, though, this Hebrew word appears in the plural, not the singular. It's not just one action or behavior on the battlefield of life that is worthy of being blessed or that makes us happy. Many actions make a person praiseworthy and happy. Countless actions strengthen and fortify us in the trials and tribulations that confront us.

So the very first word of this prayer book aims to inspire and encourage us. You are blessed, you are happy, you are praiseworthy, when you follow the strategies and tactics in this prayer book.

Then, like a good reconnaissance briefing, the psalm immediately tells us the location of the landmines. Just as an IED in Iraq can kill or disable a soldier, sin, wickedness, and mockery can disable you for life, indeed for all eternity. The psalm says, "Do not walk in the counsel of the wicked. Do not stand in the way of sinners." While wickedness and sinfulness are seldom defined in our current culture, the scriptures are less constrained. To give just one example, St. Paul in his letter to Timothy fires off a list of sins, such as being "lovers of self, lovers of money, proud, arrogant, abusive, ungrateful, unholy, inhuman, slanderers, treacherous, swollen with conceit, lovers of pleasure rather than lovers of God, even holding the form of religion but denying its power" (2 Timothy 3:2-5).

Verse 1 concludes its reconnaissance sweep of the battlefield with the warning, "Do not sit in the seat of mockers." Mockery is sometimes subtle, but it refers to those who laugh at what is holy and scorn what is divine while arrogantly claiming they know the truth. As John Calvin, the founder of the Presbyterian tradition states, you mock God when you seek to replace the Word of God with your own version of truth.[2]

Verse 2 is in total contrast to the warning in verse 1: "The praiseworthy person finds delight in the law of the Lord and on this law you meditate day and night." To David, the law of the Lord refers specifically to the law of Moses, the Torah, the first five books of the Bible: Genesis, Exodus, Leviticus, Numbers, and Deuteronomy. In fact, those were the only books, written 400 years before David, that David had in his Bible. During the thousand-year period from David to Jesus, the law of the Lord grew to include the rest of what Christians call the Old Testament. When the Risen Christ tells us to read the law of Moses, the prophets, and the psalms, He has directed us to study and delight in all of this literature, the whole of our Bible. Blessed is the person who finds his or her delight in the Bible.

The person who delights in meditating on the Bible is like a "tree planted beside streams of water" and is someone who prospers. This is the first of the two promises in this psalm. The metaphor of the "tree" is very interesting. But before exploring it, I would note that we pursue those activities which delight us and I would raise the question: What do you read and study that delights you? You can't delight in something you seldom read. What you read shows your priorities. Hopefully, reading the Bible ranks high on your personal agenda.

Back to the tree planted by streams of water. The tree is a symbol used throughout scripture. (Did you notice that "trees" are mentioned more frequently in the Garden of Eden story than "fruit"?) In the context of this psalm, a tree clearly carries the sense of absorbing and being nourished from the roots. From the depths of our being, we are encouraged to draw upon the writings of Moses, prophets like Amos and Isaiah, the wisdom in the Book of Proverbs and Ecclesiastes, the insights of Paul and Peter and John, and, of course, the Gospels.

All of this may be obvious from just reading the plain text of the passage in English. But the literal Hebrew translation is not "a tree *planted* by streams of water" but "a tree *re-planted* beside streams of water."[3] Consider how wickedness, sinfulness, and false stories that mock scripture thrive in our current environment. To avoid them, we need to be *re-planted*, even *transplanted*. As Jesus said, "You must be born again!" (John 3:3). We must resist the worldly passions that swirl around us and, by the work of the Holy Spirit, become re-planted immigrants in the environment of the Bible. This idea of re-planting also implies the assurance that the Holy Spirit continually seeks to restore us when we are withering from our relapses into sin and wickedness.

Psalm 1 concludes, as it began, with a grand promise: "For the Lord *watches* over the way of the righteous" (v.6). The Hebrew word for "watches" can also be translated as "attentive" or "to know." This verse then becomes: "The Lord *knows* the way of the righteous."

Meditate on that. David, the warrior, prompted by the Holy Spirit, proclaims a central, defining attribute of God, that God knows. God is a brain. God is *the* brain. The Creator God connects to us from God's brain to our brain. God's intellect tracks our intellect. The reciprocal is also true. When we exercise our intelligence by seeking to live in the environment of Biblical wisdom, then we extend our limited wisdom into God's and we allow God's wisdom to inform ours.

It gets even more personal. The Hebrew word for "know" and its Greek equivalent (the Hebrew scripture was translated into the Greek in what we call the Septuagint) refers to the intelligent comprehension of one who grasps something, not just observes it.

God embraces you. When you study and meditate on the word of God, the spirit of Christ permeates even to the cellular level of your brain.

Here on life's battlefield, what a comfort, what a delight, what a promise! God—the Risen Christ—knows you! And you increase your knowledge of Him. What a blessed way to live!

10

# From Despair to Exaltation

"My God, my God, why have you forsaken me?" (Psalm 22:1).

"Posterity will serve Him!" (Psalm 22:30).

This psalm starts with David's cry of feeling abandoned by God and resonates with most of us. At least on some occasions, we've faced circumstances when we, too, have cried out and asked, "Why is God so far from helping me, so far from my groaning?"

The Hebrew word for "groaning" is the same word used to describe the roar of a lion. David is a soldier who had known guerilla warfare even in his teens. He has bellowed orders to thousands in the chaos of battle. He's a combat-hardened warrior, who has thrust his sword through the belly of hundreds of opponents. He's heard their screams of agony. Now he's in the middle of the combat zone again. Surrounded by enemies, he feels abandoned and angry. David is not whimpering in a corner that God has left him. He *roars* like a wounded lion, "My God, my God, why have you forsaken me?!"

Jesus prays this very psalm on the cross, where he is nailed into paralysis and able only to move His lips. Do you think Jesus said these words with any less passion than David?

And Jesus is not reciting just the first line of the psalm. He was praying the *entire* psalm. When the Gospels quote only the first verse, it's a necessary literary device (Mark 15:34 and Matthew 27:46). For example, if you read that someone prayed, "Our Father, who art in heaven," at a graveside service, you would assume the people had said the entire Lord's Prayer, not just the first phrase.

Jesus prayed this whole psalm on the cross not only for His own comfort but also for our benefit. He's telling us, really directing us, to

Psalm 22 so that we can better understand His situation and better cope with our own.

Let's first look at the psalm in its overall context.

There is no readily agreed-upon order for the 150 psalms. They do not follow, for example, a chronological order or thematic order. They do share a fundamental orientation toward praising God. (Only Psalm 88 is pessimistic throughout, ending on a depressing note. Jesus likely prayed Psalm 88 the night He was arrested and anticipated torture.) Bundled together, the psalms cover the range of human emotion and experience, but not in a straight line.

Some psalms, however, seem to form a unit, which is possibly the case with Psalms 20, 21, 22, and 23.

In Psalms 20 and 21, David realizes that God grants him his "heart's desire" (Psalms 20:5 and 21:3). These two psalms promise David victory over his enemies and assure him that God answers when he calls. But Psalm 22 is like falling off a cliff. David abruptly goes from "We will sing and praise your power" (Psalm 21:14) to roaring, "Why have you forsaken me?!" (Psalm 22:1).

David left specific instructions for singing Psalm 22. The tiny print that appears before the first verse in many translations reveals his instructions for the choirmaster: "Set this psalm to the tune of *The Doe of the Dawn*." The musical score for this tune has yet to be recovered, so we can take some liberty to conjecture how it sounded.

I hear this composition open with a chaotic cacophony. Screaming, jeering, cursing crowds. Taunts of mockery for believing in God in the first place. Strong bulls of Bashan snorting and stomping. (Bashan was a lush pastureland noted for its livestock.) David is being attacked by enemies who charge like enraged bulls and chase him like rabid dogs and ravenous lions. David knows, and we know, that bulls gore, dogs bite, and lions eat meat. David's enemies intend to destroy and devour him. He can no longer outfight or outrun them. He's pinned down with no chance of escape. Our war veterans especially may find much in these images that speaks to them.

In the first 21 verses of the psalm, David alternates between desperation and a search for deliverance. He staggers between "God, you are not answering me!" and "Our ancestors trusted in you and you delivered them." Hopelessness is his emotional companion: "I am a worm. Scorned. Despised." David articulates the pit of despair with powerful metaphors that convey his low self-esteem. Those of us with chronic illness or who have lost jobs or didn't get the contract we bid on or the promotion we felt we deserved, might identify.

David searches his childhood experiences for comfort. David remembers how safe he felt when he clung to his mother. Those of us who have been blessed with loving, caring, and protective parents easily identify with this sentiment. But David realizes what every person at some point learns: Neither our mother nor our father, as much as they love us, can always protect us. Raucous music crashes back into the psalm.

Reading Psalm 22 closely, you realize it's divided into two parts. David's emotional and spiritual turbulence fills the first 21 verses. Then there is a dramatic shift in tone. Depending upon your translation, it occurs either in the middle of verse 21 or the start of verse 22. Both translations are correct and ultimately it doesn't make any difference. The point is the same: The second part of the psalm exudes an entirely different mood from the first part.

There's a gigantic gap between the two sections.

The first section ends with wild dogs and evil doers and raging lions. It's a battlefield with no sign of victory in sight. Suddenly the second part gazes into the future and bursts out with confident and ever-expanding praise. The praise starts with David sharing his deliverance with his family (brothers and sisters) and then expands to include his entire nation. It escalates with mounting crescendo. As if transported through the telescope of time and with eyes brightened by the Holy Spirit, David foresees that someday the Lord will rule over all the nations! David proclaims that victory to all future generations. And not only to future generations. Even the dead will rise up—only to bow down to God in awed wonder. David has whirled from humiliation to glorification, from tribulation to triumph, from woe to worship.

What happened? What happened in the gap that propelled David from feeling distant from God to feeling embraced by God?

David gives us an important clue in addressing his audience near the start of the second section, on thanksgiving: "You who *fear* the Lord, praise the Lord" (v.24). It might seem strange that the word "fear" occurs here and does not occur in the first section of the psalm. Even when he's assailed by savage enemies and near defeat in the first part of the psalm, there's no mention of fear. David reserves his fear for God. Recall that "fear" in the Bible has either of two meanings. It's "fear" as in being afraid, an emotion we all know, or "fear" in the sense of "awe" or "wonder." David is not afraid of the enemy. He does feel awe and wonder toward God.

Clearly something happened to David that answered to his prayer for strength and deliverance (v.19-21). He just doesn't give us specific details. Maybe friendly chariots came riding to his rescue. Maybe the spear hurled at him narrowly missed. Whatever it was, David praised God for the result.

I know, and you know, many people who will say with fervor equal to David's that they barely missed catastrophe, and they give God the credit. The pathology report came back with good news. The car swerved away at the last second. The check arrived just in time. But we also know countless instances where the reverse was the case. Life does not routinely bring fairy tale endings. As we all know, not everyone gains a sense of victory. For some of us some of the time, and for others of us most of the time, the gap between despair and exaltation is too severe to overcome. This is tragic, but true. We can never really know the dangers another perceives, or the depression another suffers, or the burdens another bears.

We can, however, help lift the burden. That's the model Jesus gives us. You only need to read the account of His life and how He spent His days to arrive at that conclusion. He touched people who were hurting. He healed people who were sick. He fed people who were hungry.

One of my most poignant memories from numerous times videotaping in the Dominican Republic occurred in an especially blighted area. I was interviewing an American nurse on a volunteer mission. We were in a dilapidated hut barely reachable by jeep where she knelt beside an injured boy, bandaging his wound. "Why are you doing this?" I asked her. "This is what Jesus did," she said simply. "And I want to be like Jesus." Of course, we help people. This is what Jesus did. We don't need any grand theology to follow His example.

But I'm still intrigued by the gap. How do we move—as an individual or as a church or as a nation—from despair to praising Christ? I think it has to be a miracle, albeit a miracle that takes place in the historical arena and often at the cost of flesh and blood.

Several years ago my wife, Gail, and I visited Omaha Beach in Normandy, France. This is where American troops suffered exceptionally high casualties on D-Day but eventually secured the beach for the Allied invasion. It may not be farfetched to say that if we Americans had lost that battle in 1944, France would still be under Nazi occupation and the United States would not exist. I gathered a handful of sand and let it run through my fingers. I thought of the American blood that once flooded those beaches. The thousands who died that day had roared out to have their soul delivered from the bayonet and their lives from the mouths of Nazi cannons.

They died in the gap. But their song of victory continues. All the ends of the earth remember what they did. They died in order that posterity will live.

So did Jesus. Remember, this is the psalm that Jesus prayed on the cross, the psalm that begins, "Why have you forsaken me?" What happened to Jesus when He cried out for deliverance? Nothing. At least not for three days. And we'll never know the nature of the transformation that occurred in the tomb just before Easter dawn. We just believe that His prayer—to have His precious life delivered from the sting of death—was answered, and He gained the victory (1 Corinthians 15:55). We've been celebrating that victory for over 2,000 years.

Which is not to suggest that the battles we face and the challenges that confront us are in any way mitigated. The past makes possible this moment—we praise the valor of those who died on Normandy's beaches, just as we celebrate the day of Resurrection—but these times are perilous.

More than a half-century after D-Day, former Secretary of State Henry Kissinger remarked before a Senate committee:

> We are living through a moment of monumental world change. We haven't faced such diverse crises since the end of the Second World War...The Cold War was more dangerous, [the] current times are more complicated.[4]

We can agree. We are in the gap, between the wild dogs and raging lions set on devouring us and a fouled environment foreboding extinction. Psalm 22 gives us courage to overcome our fear. Just as David praised God for his deliverance 3,000 years ago and Jesus proclaimed it 2,000 years ago, we today can still sing God's praises.

This is our privilege as Christians. It is also our responsibility as American Christians—to move beyond our angst, to try and live like Jesus, to sing God's praises. Let's do this for future generations, for people not yet born.

# Your Best Protection

"You prepare a table before me" (Psalm 23:5).

The first time I saw a real shepherd was on Mount Scopus, a hill beside the Mount of Olives on the outskirts of Jerusalem. It's 1976. My wife and I were leading a small group of pilgrims from my congregation in San Francisco to Israel. We had arrived at our hotel at night after a long and exhausting flight. Nonetheless, I was so energized by being in the Holy Land that I awakened with the first glimmer of light and went outside for a morning walk.

The area at that time was still somewhat barren, the border between countryside and city, overlooking what had until recently been designated as "no man's land." Just a few years earlier, Jerusalem had been a divided city and this area had been the scene of fierce conflict.

Then out of the stillness, I heard it: tiny ringing bells and what might have been a whistle. Squinting in the grey-pink dawn, I saw, about 25 yards away, a shepherd leading a dozen sheep down the hill.

He was filthy! Every Sunday School picture of a shepherd boy in a well pressed robe, leaning thoughtfully on his staff and gazing fondly over his lily-white lambs: shattered. Memories of all those Christmas pageants where kids dressed in bathrobes and acted as shepherds: erased. Seeing a genuine shepherd doing his daily work eradicated those imaginary images.

Biblical passages actually provide accurate descriptions of the reality of the shepherd's life, not fictional images. While we often read in the Christmas passage, "And there were shepherds living out in the fields nearby, keeping watch over their flocks at night" (NIV, Luke 2:8), the literal translation says, "And shepherds were in the same country living in the fields and *keeping guard, guard* in the night over their flock." The same Greek word for "guard" is used twice, first as a participle, then as a noun.

What new insight does the literal translation give us? It underscrores the fact that shepherds were on high alert throughout the night, just as David had been 1,000 years before the birth of Jesus. A shepherd had to be doubly alert because sheep are the most helpless of all livestock. I mean, have you ever heard a lamb even growl? Sheep cannot do anything but run. The sheep's safety depends entirely upon the shepherd.

When David wrote this psalm, he had no illusions about either the scaredy-cat nature of sheep or the need for a strong shepherd. He knew from experience, as the youngest brother assigned to the lowliest tasks, that the shepherd's life was dirty. There were no showers in the hills. It was degrading. Cleaning mud and dung from sheep was not considered a high-profile career choice. A shepherd's life was also dangerous. Snakes, wolves, lions, bears, and buzzards abounded. If the sheep were unattended even for a moment, disaster could strike. Sheep depend on the shepherd's character—not his wardrobe (Matthew 9:36).

We love to recite and repeat this familiar psalm. Funeral homes hand it out on cards. Ministers read it at virtually every funeral service. Yet the closest many of us have been to a lamb is the dinner menu at a restaurant. For that reason, the images in the psalm which refer to specific shepherd activities seem hazy for most of us. Let's look at these images in their original setting to discover what they were and ideally to make them more meaningful in our own lives. Let's not embalm the psalm, preserving it for primarily reading at funerals.

"The Lord is my shepherd" starts the psalm and "I will live in the house of the Lord forever" concludes it. From its first phrase to its last, David's images detail for us the full range of the sheep's experience under the shepherd's care. Every image shows the relationship of the sheep to the shepherd.

David places himself as one of the sheep. It's rather surprising that David portrays himself as the weak lamb, not a robust shepherd. And David is no wimp. He's lived in the hills, made campfires without matches, and faced death with the regularity of a Navy SEAL. "Standing guard" he chased away wolves and killed lions to protect his lambs. The Bible calls him the Shepherd-King. He's the army general of his people. But surprise!

David's opening salute is total humility: The Lord is *my* shepherd! I'm not the great protector and provider. God is.

"I shall not want," verse 1 continues. David doesn't say, "God will keep me in luxury." This psalm eviscerates the 'prosperity Gospel' we hear from television's so-called Christian preachers and radio's so-called evangelists. The shepherd's psalm—along with the rest of the Bible—says, "Trust God to provide for your needs, not fulfill your greed."

"He makes me lie down in green pastures" (v.2). Israel is not a desert. Though there are deserts within its borders and it is for the most part an arid land, there are spots of rich vegetation. David is tending his sheep around Bethlehem, a hilly and a rocky area. Finding the lush, green pastures required advance knowledge of the terrain on the part of the shepherd.

Sheep are notoriously reluctant to "lie down."[5] They are not just extremely timid and therefore easily frightened. They are tormented by insects because they lack a tail long enough to swat away gnats and flies. While the morning dew on lush grass can satisfy their thirst for a day, sheep can't dig for water.

Sheep are also clumsy. They stumble and fall down, or they roll over and can't get up without help. Lying on their back, bleating helplessly, their little legs beating the air, sheep who are "cast down" can die within hours unless the shepherd rescues them. When a shepherd sees buzzards circling overhead, he will race to that area, hoping to arrive before the lion or the bear.

Sheep need to be guided on the "right path," an acceptable translation for "paths of righteousness" (v.3). But sheep can be stubborn, prone to wander off by themselves and get lost. Jesus refers to this trait in the parable of the shepherd who leaves his flock to search for the one who is lost (Luke 15:3). One way the shepherd seeks lost sheep is by whistling. In the Book of Judges, the writer castigates shepherds who just sit safely by the campfire rather than go off into the night and whistle for the lost sheep (Judges 5:16).

David summarizes this first section of the psalm with the phrase, "He restores my soul" (v.3). More literally he's saying, "The shepherd restores my *life*." By strong implication he's saying, "Even though the Lord has provided green pastures and sufficient nourishment and right paths, I have wandered and strayed like a lost sheep. I am spiritually in danger and I need to be saved." David experienced moments like this in his life when he himself deeply knew that he needed to be set aright.

Have you ever felt that way? Have you ever had the sense that perhaps the Lord had offered you a path with "green pastures," but that you—for whatever reasons or by whatever temptations—had turned aside and missed that mark?

Let me suggest that the psalms themselves can serve as your green pastures. Go to them. Graze in them. In the dew of the morning find a drop of spiritual moisture that will sustain you through the day. Listen for the soft whistle of a phrase from a psalm which, like a shepherd, is searching...for you.

The middle section of this psalm becomes very personal. It goes from the third person, "He leads me" in verse 3 to the second person, "You are with me. You comfort me" in verse 4. The sheep can sense when they are in dangerous situations. They've been led out of the sheep pen into the hills. They've left their comfort zone and find themselves in a land with no street lights. But they trust their shepherd.

Because the shepherd has a weapon. That's the "rod" in the phrase, "Your rod and your staff, they comfort me" (v.4). The rod is a small club, made from a tree branch, which a shepherd may cut and carve to his or her own specifications. (Females were also shepherds, as Genesis 29:9 indicates.) They used the rod to pummel a poisonous snake or perhaps hurl at a wolf.

The rod was also, however, a source of comfort to the sheep. When the shepherd would count (Ezekiel 20:37) and inspect the sheep, he might use the rod to hold a sheep in place or use the rod to push back the thick wool as he searched for cuts or bruises.

"Know the conditions of your flock" is a phrase in Proverbs 27:23 that refers to this activity. The shepherd knows the conditions of the flock by having them pass, one by one, under his rod, as he counts and measures and inspects them.

We experience something analogous in our lives in business, in school, in church, and at home.

- In business, we need to know the conditions of the enterprise: the exact count of our inventory, the detail in our Excel spreadsheets, the accuracy of our budgets, up-to-date contact information on our prospects, and the frequency with which we've contacted customers. These facts, figures, and other data are "passing under the rod" of the owner or managers because it is essential for them to know the conditions of the flock.

- Teachers speak to, and may even touch, the children under their care. They greet them as they enter the class at the start of the day. They're counting them. They're reassuring them. Teachers are taking care of their little lambs.

- Ministers and church officers need to know the conditions of the congregation from the state of the building to the care of each member, from the details of the budget to the purpose and effectiveness of the mission and its faithfulness to the Gospel. Each part of church life passes under the rod of the leaders of that community.

- Every parent, spouse, and guardian who experiences strained relationships, or who has children with substance issues, or who has lost a loved one, yearns for the sense of comfort and care this psalm offers.

The rod of the Lord can also serve as a metaphor for the Word of the Lord. The Word of the Lord comforts you. Every psalm has a word, a phrase, a sentence, that can speak to you when you most need it. "Come to Me," Jesus says. "and I will give you rest" (Matthew 11:28). Quite often that "rest" from the Lord comes to us through the psalms.

The "rod of the Lord" that comforts is also the Word of the Lord that scrutinizes. Have you ever felt "inspected" by the Word, when a passage gets so inside your brain that it pierces your thoughts with an intensity sharper than a two-edged sword (Hebrews 4:12)?

Has the Word of the Lord served as a protective weapon for you, when you hurled it at temptation as if into the face of Satan himself? That's exactly how Jesus used the Word when He faced temptation. "It is written!" He said in response to each temptation (Luke 4:1-13 and Matthew 4:1-11).

The valleys of life and the shadow of death (v.4) seem to be where we often find our greatest assurance of the Lord's presence. It's helpful to realize that nothing in a *shadow* can harm us. You can't even really touch a shadow. There is no there, there. The only reason we see a shadow is because there is a light, and the light controls the shadows. That's a primary lesson in learning photography: The light source controls the shadows.

Light is an important metaphor throughout the psalms (Psalms 27:1, 37:6, 43:3, 49:19, 97:11, 119:105 and 130, and 139:12, for example), a metaphor which Jesus appropriates. He makes the audacious claim that He is the Light of the world. As the Light, He can control the shadows.

Does that mean only a 'feel good' sort of placebo effect that doesn't really change the underlying condition? When I had a stroke, did the effects of the stroke totally disappear? No. After my knee replacement, could I then run a marathon or even run to the corner? Not hardly. After my father died suddenly from pancreatic cancer, was not the grief profound? Even though my mother transitioned to heaven after her full three score years and ten, do I not still yearn for her presence?

The reality is that life includes challenges, hardships, and loss. Valleys with deep shadows creep over our world today. It's all too common that self-proclaimed Christians support very un-Jesus-like politicians and personalities whose policies and practices Jesus would scorn. The poor are increasingly marginalized and our nation's doors are callously slammed shut. Shadows fall on the most vulnerable people while Christians hide the Light of Christ under bushels of fear, greed, and selfishness.

What Light of Christ helps illumine your way? What Word of the Lord inspires you, that you might assist and encourage others?

"You prepare a table before me, in the presence of my enemies. You anoint my head with oil. My cup overflows" (v.5). King David was a former shepherd, not a chef. In the context of this psalm, the "oil" and "cup" refer to the care of the sheep. When the sheep get small cuts or infections, the shepherd rubs soothing oil into the wounds. A cup is a container with set limits but, in this psalm, the shepherd's cup of oil is overflowing. It's running over. It's saturating the sheep. Do you sense the Good Shepherd's cup of care overflowing for you?

In videotaping for Christian medical mission groups in some of the poorest barrios in our hemisphere, I have often observed the Good Shepherd's overflowing cup of care. It bears little relationship to a person's physical health or financial well-being. The large tent quickly erected in Haiti was filled with hundreds of people displaced by a natural disaster. On canes and crutches and clutching the only clothes they had, they sang with vibrancy and conviction, "O Lord, my God, when I in awesome wonder...." They were living in a "valley" and "shadow" moment, but they saw a Light that enlightened me. And many clients who receive a simple free lunch at the Neighborhood Center in Camden, New Jersey, where I volunteer, routinely say "God bless you" as they enter and "I am so blessed" as they leave. Yes, they would be better off with a job or a pension or health insurance. But they seem to walk in a high-crime shadow environment with a firm and grateful confidence in their Good Shepherd.

My observation is that the Spirit of Jesus often saturates people whose financial means are modest or meager with blessings about which many of us in middle- and upper-class America are ignorant. Not that we miss out entirely on blessings, by any means. But to the extent that we share in them, it's despite our material comforts, not because of them. As the Rev. Eugene Farlough (of blessed memory) once observed, rich people were seldom the best friends of Jesus. In one noteworthy instance, one prominent citizen saved his admiration for Jesus to the very end, providing His crucified body with a tomb (referring to Nicodemus, John 19:38-42).

The table in this psalm is not a dinner table. It refers to the plateau areas around Bethlehem. When David writes, "You prepare a table before me" (v.5), he's indicating that the shepherd goes ahead of the sheep, out of the valley, up the mountain, to prepare pasture on the plateau for his sheep. The shepherd is on the lookout for wild animals and surveys the area for poisonous snakes or toxic weeds that would threaten the flock. The point is that the shepherd is the advance guard who scouts out the pasture—preparing and making ready the table—for the sheep.

Using these concrete images grounded in the practical activities of daily life, David the psalmist assures us that God is going ahead of us in the events of our day. The Lord is preparing the people you're to meet or the circumstances you might encounter. Jesus Christ, our Good Shepherd, is preparing you, and them, in advance, for how your day unfolds.

Let me give a personal example. I don't see myself as a particularly brave man, primarily because I am not a brave man. I have needed to trust in the Good Shepherd as I've videotaped in remote areas in Haiti and the

Dominican Republic. Sometimes I had to do this work in potentially dangerous situations.

In 2010 I was part of a small group that flew into Port au Prince just a few months after Haiti's disastrous earthquake. I was accompanying Foundation for Peace staff and volunteers who were there to help build a small school and medical clinic. My job was to produce a fundraising and volunteer recruitment video.

Port au Prince and its environs were in a state of collapse. The earthquake had devastated a country that already lacked a functioning government and critical infrastructure. The airport's arrival terminal resembled a barren hangar. Barbed wire surrounded the parking lot to keep both the begging homeless and the preying criminal element away from arriving passengers.

We didn't leave the airport area for our destination, about 50 miles away, until it was already dark. Ten of us were crammed into the back of a dilapidated pick-up truck. Outside Port au Prince, there were no lights. Anywhere. Because there was no electricity. Anywhere. Every eight or ten minutes we could see what might have been a lantern or a candle. As we drove into the darkness, there were no other head lights or tail lights, because there was no other traffic. Our truck had only one headlight. There were no stars, which seemed to fit the foreboding mood, as dark clouds threatened storms.

We were driving on what had barely been a road even before the earthquake and now was an obstacle course of potholes, fallen trees, and flooded-out sections. Clutching my camera bag in my lap, I could just make out a man a few feet away riding with us in the bed of the pick-up, gripping a pistol in his lap. As we bounced along, all of us pretty much in silence, I remember thinking to myself, "I wonder if we're being kidnapped." Then I sort of reassured myself by thinking, "No, this truck is more likely to plunge into a ravine." So much for deep spiritual thoughts.

As the ride continued, I realized that whatever was going on was totally out of my control, and I remembered a scene from back at the airport. We had been greeted by an incredibly charismatic Haitian who assured us that he had gone before us and that there were people waiting to receive us. I found myself relaxing, filled with confidence that this man had prepared the way and that everything we needed would be ready for us.

In retrospect I can say that he was our shepherd. In the middle of Haiti, after an earthquake, in the dark, I was in "green pastures."

If you get anything at all from this reflection on Psalm 23, here's the take-away:

Don't put off using this psalm until your funeral. You won't be there anyway.

Use it now.

Live it now.

Apply it now.

Don't leave home without it.

# The Best Experience Yet

"Taste and see that the Lord is good" (Psalm 34:8).

Psalm 34 is an action-packed poem written by David, one of the world's greatest warriors, one of the Bible's best-known personalities, and its most famous king. David wrote this psalm after surviving several near-death experiences. His life at this time was in even greater danger than when he killed the giant Goliath in a one-on-one fight. This psalm takes place when he may have been on the home turf of Goliath's relatives, who were seeking revenge.[6]

Bringing Goliath's brothers into this biblical scene draws upon a colorful interpretation from Jewish scholars of the short descriptive synopsis of the psalm, which is written in small print in some Bibles, just before verse 1: "A psalm of David, when he feigned madness before Abimelech." Abimelech was a title for the Philistine king of Gath, who ruled a hostile neighboring kingdom, as described in 1 Samuel 21.

To better understand the psalm—and, in doing so, to encourage you to return to it frequently as part of your own prayer life—let's first consider its structure.

This psalm is what's known as an acrostic in that it follows the Hebrew alphabet. The first letter of each verse starts with the letters of the Hebrew alphabet in order (with the exception of verse 6). Imagine an English poem where the first stanza starts with 'A,' the second stanza 'B,' and so forth.

This structure helps highlight the psalm's central theme, which is announced in verse 1 with the first Hebrew letter *aleph*: "I will bless the Lord at all times." Then the psalm enumerates the variety of circumstances to which the phrase "at all times" applies. Just as every letter of the alphabet is necessary for the structure of language, so too is it important to praise

God in every circumstance.[7] You can't leave even one event in your life out of your praise of God any more than you can leave one letter out of the alphabet. In each event of your life—times of troubles and times of deliverance, times of fear and times of joy—bless and praise the Lord. That's the main message of the psalm.

Praising God at all times in every situation is not easy. Actually, I would say it's impossible. The impossibility of praising God in every episode is implied in the psalm. That is, it's impossible if we rely on our own strength and abilities to do so.

That's the point in verse 2 of the psalm where David says, "My soul boasts in the Lord." David is not boasting or glorifying himself or his own accomplishments. In our culture of 'selfies,' this may be difficult for us to grasp, especially when we consider how truly impressive David's credentials were.

There was much David could have bragged about. As a teenager armed only with a slingshot, he kills the giant Goliath and leads the Israelites to victory. He's so successful in battle that the people compose songs to praise him. He becomes the son-in-law of King Saul and essentially the king's chief bodyguard and head of the secret service. A prophet predicts that David himself will become king. In short, before he's 30 years old David has amassed a resume that George Washington or Winston Churchill might envy. Does David extol himself over these exploits? No, he boasts only that he is a servant whom God has blessed and saved.

David views every aspect of his life—from A to Z—under the providence of God. Therefore, he can say, "I will bless the Lord at all times." Let me suggest that only when we see every circumstance in our lives as under the providence of God and led by Jesus Christ can we, too, say, "I will bless the Lord at all times."

There were many occasions in David's life, however, when he was *not* willing to praise God and David also makes that fact plain in this psalm. The realization of his shortcomings may well be what prompted him to write the psalm. There's an inherent tension in the psalm as David wants to praise God at all times yet realizes he himself did not.

Consider, for example, David's lack of faith, a subtle point that we notice in the Old Testament passage which provides the context for this psalm (1 Samuel 21). "Blessed is the man who takes refuge in the Lord,"

David writes poetically in Psalm 34:8. But when David as a hungry and defenseless refugee running for his life initially met the priest at Nob, he almost immediately asks, "Do you have a weapon?" Faced with danger, his first thought is to find refuge in the defense industry. The priest gives him the sword of Goliath, carefully wrapped in the priest's trophy case. "There's no other sword like it!" David exclaims, and we can imagine him swinging it around as many of us would do if we held it. But that esteemed sword had not saved its original owner. When Goliath the gladiator hoisted it, David the shepherd rendered it harmless.

David had trusted that God would give him strength to defeat any enemy in those days. Back then, all he needed was one pebble and a slingshot because he found his refuge in God (a major point of 1 Samuel 17). Now, just a few years later, he has mislaid that faith. This psalm's title tells us David suffered momentary insanity before the Philistine king. David also suffered momentary faithlessness when he praises the sword of Goliath, an item which David himself had doomed to defeat.

Isn't this a warning to all of us: that whatever our age or past exploits, we might falter? David may sense this truth and seeks to atone for his shortcomings by starting this psalm by saying, "I *shall* bless the Lord at all times!" In retrospect, he wishes he had. If he had to do it over again, he would—which is perhaps why it's now the letter 'A' in his acrostic psalm. Some of us can identify with David's sentiments. The devotion to Jesus that we may have once known did not always burn as brightly in all the circumstances of life as we would want. Looking back, we like David want a re-do. Looking ahead, we hope to say with David, "In the future, I will bless the Lord at all times!"

While David writes in verse 13, "Keep your lips from telling lies," he himself tells a lie when he encountered the priest at Nob. "Give me some food. I left in such a hurry to carry out the mission of the king I didn't have time to stop by the royal kitchen and grab a bite to eat." Hardly. He wasn't on a mission *for* the king. He was escaping *from* the king. But he was convincing enough that the priest believed him.

This lie may seem justified because David was saving himself from unjust persecution, but it had devastatingly catastrophic consequences. As we read in 1 Samuel 22, after learning that David had gone to the priest at Nob, King Saul was convinced that there was a conspiracy against him.

(In some respects, he was correct.) In his homicidal rage, Saul not only has that priest killed but slaughters a total of 85 priests. He doesn't stop there. Saul channels the power of evil and destroys the entire town—women, children, livestock. This chapter reads like the rampage of butchery across the Middle East today, or the Holocaust in Europe, or the slaughter of Native Americans, lynching of African-Americans, and the mass shootings on school grounds in this country, to mention just a few massacres that pockmark more recent history.

How can we make sense of such butchery? We can't. But we can seek to resist and prevent it. The Bible shows that in this instance the slaughter had its roots in a lie. David had fabricated a seemingly innocuous story in order to save his own life. Many ethical people would likely say, "Sure, go ahead. Tell a small lie in order to save yourself or to get some food or advance in your business or in school. No big deal." No harm, no foul, as we used to say on the basketball courts back in Indiana.

This Bible story contends with uncomfortable clarity that a small lie can have staggeringly large consequences. Since Satan is described as the Father of Lies (John 8:44), it should be evident to us as Christians that lies serve Satan's purposes. We are so immersed in a culture that cultivates lying and half-truths that we cannot fathom the danger in little so-called white lies. But a lie is a lie is a lie. Even small lies can become weapons of mass destruction.

David had as much trouble with this as we do, which is why he warns us in verse 13, "Come, listen to me. Do you want to enjoy life and enjoy good days? Then keep your tongue from evil and your lips from speaking lies." He's not writing this from a pedestal of self-righteousness. He wrote it because he carried the guilt of the slaughter of the innocents like a backpack laden with bricks. He's pleading with us. "Take it from me. Don't lie."

David obviously made mistakes, but these are not his defining moments. They are part of the whole alphabet of his life; they are not the definition of his life. Note that the "sword of Goliath" in which he once trusted now disappears from the biblical record. In this psalm, David teaches us that those who learn the fear of the Lord (v.11)—which is to say, those who seek to obey Him, to seek peace, and to pursue it—are now identified as the "righteous" in the eyes of God. God sees them as righteous even though, as David testifies, their righteousness derives not from the sum total of their actions but from their fear of God.

We seek to praise God at all times even with our imperfections. As the poet and songwriter Leonard Cohen writes, "Ring the bells that still can ring./Forget your perfect offering./There is a crack in everything./That's how the light gets in."[8] The light of prophecy provided by the Holy Spirit inspired David in this psalm to lift the future's curtain and anticipate the cross of Christ. The psalm ends:

Yahweh Himself ransoms the souls of His servants.

Those who take shelter in Him will not be condemned (v.23).

David's psalm is prophetic. A thousand years after he wrote it, we believe that God ransomed Himself for us through the medium of Jesus on the cross. In the unfathomable economy of God, the crucified Jesus paid the ransom to free us from the Father of Lies. Because of the cross, God looks upon us and does not see us in our failures. God views imperfect believers through the divine filter of the blood of Jesus and sees us—sees you—as righteous. Surely the Lord is good!

# The Peaceable Kingdom

"The wicked will be no more but the meek shall
possess the land" (Psalm 37:10-11).

When the Quaker minister, Edward Hicks, painted *The Peaceable Kingdom* in 1826, he could not have imagined that it would become one of the most familiar images in American culture. Since Hicks painted 62 versions of the picture, you likely have seen it. You probably sensed that the theological beliefs Hicks portrays through his art are as timely now as they were in 1826. But you may have seldom considered how those beliefs draw directly from Psalm 37 and are embedded in the preaching of Jesus.

Search for *The Peaceable Kingdom Painting* on the internet. I especially like the one located at the Philadelphia Museum of Art. Notice that the painting is divided in two, demarcated by the strong brown diagonal line. The right side of the painting illustrates the vision of the prophet (Isaiah 11:6-9, echoed in Isaiah 65:25): The leopard shall lie down with the lamb, the cow and the lion together, and a little child shall lead them. The left side includes a ship resting placidly in the center of a harbor and a small cluster of people gathered under a spreading elm tree where several Native Americans and five fresh immigrants from England inspect a document. This represents William Penn signing a treaty with the Lenape Indians, which tradition says Penn negotiated when he landed in America in 1682.

The artist is visualizing the prophetic future. The lion is at peace with the lamb, alongside the seed for that prophesy being planted in the green pasture of history. Instead of war, there's the suggestion of potential racial harmony.

Even without a cross or a halo in this picture, we know it depicts spiritual tenderness and of a hopeful future for all children. The child in the painting, who could be interpreted as either a boy or girl, is clothed in white, as if illuminated from within. We can readily view the little child as a Christ figure—not unexpected, since Hicks was a Quaker minister. And for Quakers, the Inner Light of Christ is in everyone, a conviction based in St. Paul's writing that Christ Himself is in us (Colossians 1:27). The mystery of Christ in us is what many Quakers consider the Inner Light.

Does the painting capture reality as Hicks knew it in his lifetime? Clearly not. The peaceable kingdom is the world Hicks envisioned, not the world that Hicks inhabited. In 1826, the year Hicks painted this picture, the notorious Sing Sing prison was built. It's the same year the first American warship to circumnavigate the globe sailed out of the New York harbor—a rather stark contrast to the sailboat nestled sweetly in the center of this painting.

Hicks may or may not have been aware of these specific acts that contrast so starkly with his painting of earthly harmony, but he certainly felt the tremors of the times. Slavery—that can rightly be considered our country's original sin—was a divisive issue even among Quakers in Philadelphia, not to mention the rest of the country, even though it's still several decades before the Civil War. The president of the United States at the time, John Quincy Adams, was not a slaveholder but James Monroe, who preceded Adams, and Andrew Jackson, who followed him, were themselves both slave owners. In fact, of the first 12 presidents of the United States, only two never owned slaves: John Quincy Adams and his father, John Adams.

Thus, we can see that the arc of the moral universe, a poetic metaphor that enamored Martin Luther King, Jr., had not bent very far toward justice when Edward Hicks began painting pictures of a peaceable kingdom. But that did not stop him from painting the picture of the world he desired and the world he was willing to work toward.

That the world we want is not yet the world we live in is where I make the connection between Hicks' painting and Psalm 37. Just as Hicks divides his painting of the *Peaceable Kingdom* into two sections, Psalm 37 is similarly divided. The psalm is a study in contrasts that describes the conflict between the wicked and the righteous and their disparate characters and fates.

Fully 15 of the 40 verses in this psalm tell us about the wicked and the ruin that awaits them:

The wicked will fade and wither (v.1).

The wicked will be cut off (v.9).

The wicked will be no more (v.10).

The wicked plot against the righteous, gnashing their teeth (v.12).

The Lord laughs at the wicked for He sees their self-inflicted downfall (v.13).

The abundance of the wicked is ultimately no good (v.16).

The arms of the wicked will be broken (v.17).

The wicked will vanish and perish (v.20).

The wicked will borrow and go into debt (v.21).

The children of the wicked will be cut off (v.28).

The wicked seek to slay the righteous (v.32).

The wicked will be destroyed (v.34).

The wicked appear overbearing and towering but they will be no more (v.35).

The posterity of the wicked will be cut off (v.38).

The righteous will be delivered from the wicked (v.40).

While the dire consequences predicted for the wicked are not always immediately apparent, we can point to examples of their sudden and spectacular downfall. Take the case of a New York businessman who was frequently in the news for his lavish lifestyle. He brought his sons into business with him and trained them for success. Then one morning the police raided his office.

The businessman, Bernie Madoff, had run a Ponzi scheme for almost 50 years, pocketing tens of millions of dollars. Then his phony empire suddenly crashed. He was sentenced to 150 years in prison. Both of his sons died in disgrace. His wife won't talk to him or visit him. In his wickedness, the abundant wealth of this once-towering figure vanished. If the psalm is to be believed, the Lord now laughs at Bernie's self-inflicted downfall.

Psalm 37 also shows us the picture of the righteous. Verse 1 instructs us on the attitude the righteous should have: "Do not fret and do not be envious of the wicked." The most literal translation for the Hebrew word that is often translated "fret" is "contest." We are not to compete with the methods of the wicked and the wrongdoers in their arena. We're not to play their con games, in any of its myriad forms.

The psalmist prescribes the way those who seek righteousness should behave. Rather than compete with the wicked in their sordid behavior:

- Trust in the Lord and do good—do a *mitzvah*—in the Hebrew (v.3). Do a good deed for someone, regardless of how small it may appear. What seems small to you may greatly impact someone else.
- Take delight in the Lord (v.4). How do you take delight in the Lord? Attending church, listening to the music, singing hymns, hearing prayers, and enjoying the fellowship of other people are obvious examples. You take delight in the Lord when you relish the beauty and majesty of God's creation. You take delight in the Lord when you attend to the needs of the neediest.

Trusting and delighting in the Lord encompass actions and attitudes that are individualized and endlessly varied. But they share in the encircling promise that the righteous shall inherit the earth. This is a promise Jesus reiterates on the Sermon on the Mount when He quotes directly from verse 11 of Psalm 37 saying, "The meek shall inherit the earth" (Matthew 5:5).

Let's be honest. What the psalmist says and what Jesus preaches are hard to believe. In history or current affairs, it's not at all evident that the wicked will be destroyed or the meek will inherit the earth. It wasn't evident when the prophet Isaiah wrote, when Jesus preached, or when Hicks painted. It didn't work out so well for the Lenape Indians who once inhabited New Jersey and large swaths of the east coast. They didn't get the land; they got a high school named after them. Nor is the prospect of a peaceable kingdom in our immediate view. That our earth is under duress physically, politically, and spiritually is painfully clear. The science of climate change points to calamitous consequences for our environment even as the Republican Party and its leadership exit international agreements intended to mitigate the impending disaster. Wars vomit refugees fleeing torture and death. We see human flesh seared by chemical weapons yet refuse to let the sight sear our conscience. Racial hate crimes and anti-Semitic ideologies accelerate even here in America, with devastating consequences. Our polarizations are so extreme we cannot agree whether or not an 18-year-old should own a military-grade assault weapon.

But just because we live in fractious times, is that any reason not to hope for and to work for the peaceable kingdom envisioned in the painting and promised by Isaiah and Jesus?

In 1968, I was in my second year of seminary when Martin Luther King, Jr., was murdered. The peaceable kingdom was not on any horizon. During that tumultuous year, Martin Luther King, Jr. was killed; Bobby Kennedy was assassinated; the Tet Offensive happened during the height of the Vietnam War; the horrendous My Lai massacre of Vietnamese men women and children by American troops occurred; and Lyndon Johnson decided not to run for president again because of the massive anti-Vietnam War and civil rights protests. There was a lot of darkness in the world in 1968. (It was also the year that McDonald's introduced the Big Mac, so the year was not a total loss.)

In 1968 we sang *We Shall Overcome* and *This Little Light of Mine*, but many of us wondered if *any* light would make a difference. I admit: I often feel the same way now. What conceivable difference can I make—or can you make—when the world we live in is so far from the peaceable kingdom Hicks painted and Psalm 37 describes and that Jesus seems to promise us?

I don't know.

But I do know that those of us who attend church and seek to follow Jesus have no alternative but to commit our way to the Lord, to trust in Him, and to work for a better world. And in a very odd way, I'm grateful to live in these challenging times, when the imperative of seeking the peaceable kingdom and the biblical guidance for reaching it are so very clear.

Like the Quaker Edward Hicks, we are encouraged to paint, even in our older age, our distinctive picture of a peaceable kingdom for our times, adding our brushstrokes to the canvas of God's creation. Then we can hope that little children, the next generation, will do better than we do.

Which I believe is the case. In 1968, 50,000 people marched in Washington DC as part of the Poor People's March, taking up the cause that cost Martin Luther King Jr., his life. In March of 2018, hundreds of thousands of people marched in Washington DC, while tens of thousands more marched in Philadelphia and New York and Chicago and across the country, taking up the cause of gun control—an extension of the movement for which Martin Luther King, Jr. shed his blood. People of all ages and races filled the streets, walking in peaceful harmony. The speakers, none of whom was a politician, the oldest of whom was a student survivor of the Columbine shooting 19 years earlier, the youngest of whom was the 9-year-old granddaughter of Martin Luther King, Jr., inspired us. These young people organized, marched, spoke—and will vote—for a change in gun laws, for extricating our government from the disproportionate power of the NRA, for the desire to attend school or walk the streets or drive a car without the fear of being shot.

Will they succeed? Will the peaceable kingdom predicted by Isaiah, painted by Hicks, and promised by Jesus come to pass in their lifetime? That is very hard to say and the odds are likely against it. But to borrow words from a song that Marvin Gaye made popular back in 1968, "I heard it through the grapevine."

I heard it through the heavenly grapevine. Miracles happen! Keep the faith!

God in His Providence has entrusted those of us in the church today to preserve, and to encourage, the church of tomorrow.

# Seeking Good News

"Be still, and know that I am God" (Psalm 46:10).

As chaos and mayhem often threaten to overwhelm us, the poet Anne Sexton expresses our desire for peace and stability in her poem entitled *Letter Written on a Ferry While Crossing Long Island Sound*.⁹ She's in a dismal mood herself when she sees four nuns, also on the ferry, and begins to imagine them flying off, four abreast, headed for the horizon, "singing without sound." The poem's last stanza is compelling:

They are going up.
See them rise on black wings,
drinking the sky,
...They call back to us
from the gauzy edge of paradise,
Good news! Good news!

Good news. That's what the poet yearned for but didn't find this side of paradise (she committed suicide). That's what we ache to hear and want to discern in the day's frequently tumultuous events. Instead we are often bombarded with a litany of disasters.

That painful recital would not surprise the author of Psalm 46, who writes—sings, more accurately—that "God is our refuge and strength, an ever-present help in trouble" (v.1). The Hebrew word for "trouble" is actually in the plural: God is an ever-present help in troubles. The sentence can be literally translated as "God is a much-to-be-found help in troubles." The psalmist describes the troubles of his day: The environment is ripped asunder by earthquakes and floods and avalanches. Nations suffer catastrophic revolutions and governments fall. Then, in the midst of this chaotic violence, the psalmist writes, "God makes wars cease to the ends of the earth. God breaks the bow and shatters the spear and burns the shields with fire" (v.10).

Really?

Though the psalmist claims that God brings warfare to an end, history and current events continually demonstrate verse 7 of this psalm, that "nations rage and kingdoms totter" and the "earth will melt" because of human-induced climate change. A quick survey shows us the exile of the Jews in the Babylonian captivity hundreds of years before the birth of Christ, as the Bible describes, the crusaders marauding through the 11th century, a massive re-ordering of national boundaries in Europe and the Middle East during World War I, and the holocaust of World War II. Then we have the Korean War, the Vietnam War, wars in Iraq and Afghanistan, and the unwinding of the world order today. Not at all the Almighty's design. Yet in our Bible we read that "God makes wars cease to the ends of the earth."

How naive can this be? It hardly bears up under scrutiny. As one who loves biblical literature and both believes it and wants to believe it, I am not inclined toward fantasy or denial. This passage, while no doubt comforting, is simultaneously disconcerting. How am I—how are you—to understand, much less embrace, the assertion that God makes wars cease when the contrary is preeminently the case?

To help us wring meaning from Psalm 46, appreciating the psalm's context is critical. Let's start with asking who wrote this psalm. No, not David, which was probably your instinctive answer and a good guess. But David is only one of perhaps as many as ten authors of the psalms. Fortunately, it's not hard to learn who wrote this one. You only need to read English, not Hebrew. In small print in most Bibles, right under number 46, it says, "For the director of music. Of the Sons of Korah. A song."

Korah, as students of biblical history will recall, is a leader in one of the 12 tribes that are traveling with Moses in the exodus. The Israelites have miraculously crossed the Red Sea and are trekking in the wilderness, headed for the Promised Land of Israel. The tribes have clearly-assigned roles and tasks, as well as defined places in an overall organizational plan which the books of Leviticus and Numbers numbingly detail. Few people spend time pondering this organizational chart these days but knowing the tribes' roles is critical for understanding Psalm 46.

One of those tribes, the Levites, included the clan of Korah. Korah's clan had the responsibility of caring for and carrying the tent poles and curtains that would be erected around the Holy of Holies whenever the tribes set up the tabernacle in camp. Inside the Holy of Holies, behind the curtains, was the Ark of the Covenant, world history's most sacred item. While Korah and his sons had the privilege and the responsibility for the curtains and the poles, once they hung the curtains around the Ark, Korah was not allowed to enter the sacred space of the Holy of Holies and make special offerings. This privilege belonged exclusively to Aaron and his sons, the High Priests.

The special role assigned to Korah—charge of the space containing the Ark—was not enough for him.[10] He instigated a rebellion against this arrangement (Numbers 16). He enlisted 250 community leaders and together they challenged Moses' authority. Moses had claimed that God had told him exactly how the worshipping community and the people of Israel were to be governed. In their worship and in their behavior, they were to exhibit the life of holiness and faithfulness that God had ordained for them. Korah in essence said, "No, Moses. You have no special revelation from God. All of us are equally chosen by God and we have just as much right as you or Aaron or anyone else to interpret what God says. We are going to go behind the curtain into the Holy of Holies ourselves."

Moses was horrified beyond any measure that we can imagine because he knew God as you and I never can. Moses was the only person the Old Testament describes as speaking with God face-to-face. God had spoken to Moses not just once but twice in providing the Ten Commandments. Moses, who in the name of God had defeated the Pharaoh of Egypt, the most powerful man in the world, fully understood the power of God. Moses knew that you just did not mess with the authority and commands of God!

Let's step outside this story momentarily to say in another way what is happening. By questioning Moses, Korah symbolically challenges God's authority at its very root. He's not the first person in biblical history to challenge God. But Korah, the counterfeit—with the support of 250 community leaders—tries to pass himself off as a legitimate interpreter of God's authority.

We understand the role of counterfeiters and the harm they can do.

Accept counterfeit money at the bank or in a store and you are soundly cheated. Use a counterfeit medication and you could be dead. While we can appreciate the dangers inherent in counterfeit monies or medicines, we seldom consider the dangers of counterfeit theologies that carry fake biblical authority. The story of Korah is an early example of a counterfeiter attempting to usurp God's authority.

Korah's grab for power didn't work. The story is quite exciting. "If you are correct in making your power play," Moses declares to Korah and his followers, "then you will die an ordinary death. But if something dramatic happens that has never happened before, and the earth opens up like a huge sink hole and swallows you and your family, then know that you have overstepped the authority of God." At that, some people moved away from Korah. Those who did not were buried alive as the sands collapsed and Korah and his tents and his family sank into the depths.

Except for the sons of Korah! The biblical book of 2 Chronicles reports that not all the family died. And here in the Book of Psalms, we find Psalms 42 through 49 that are attributed to the sons of Korah. Perhaps three sons who are mentioned by name in the genealogical list composed them, or perhaps their progeny did, writing centuries later during the time of King David.

Whoever wrote them and whenever they were written, the spirit of inspiration pulsates through the psalms attributed to the sons of Korah. These psalms link directly back to the tragedy of Korah and the experience of the Jews described in the Book of Exodus.

The Sons of Korah saw their father disappear into a sink hole. "God is our refuge and strength," they write. "We will not fear, though the earth give way" (Psalm 46:1,3). For me, the fact that this psalm is credited to the sons of Korah helps keep it from being naive or mere fantasy. The sons of Korah had literally stood at the edge of disaster. They had found ever-present help in their time of troubles. And they had survived.

Having considered both the context of the psalm and some of its content, what is its claim on you?

- If you, like Korah, have ever refused the privileges and obligations that God has assigned to you, and thus challenged the authority of God, then the story of Korah is worthy of your attention.
- If you, like the sons of Korah, have ever found in your "time of troubles" the strength and refuge that God provides, often through the care and comfort of others, then they have written a psalm you can sing.

Listen. God Himself speaks in only *one* verse in this entire collection of psalms by the sons of Korah. From the yearning of the soul to find God in Psalm 42, to the chaos of the nations and upheaval of nature in Psalm 46, to the hint of immortality in Psalm 49, only once—in verse 10 of Psalm 46—do we hear the voice of God speak directly to the human condition.

This is what God says:

"Be still, and know that *I* am God.

*I* will be exalted among the nations, *I* will be exalted in the earth (Psalm 46:10)."

The phrase "Be still" can be an invitation for quiet meditation, an entirely appropriate interpretation. But the word can also be translated as a command: "Desist!" "Be quiet!" This might well be what God is saying to us when we mask our uncertainties and doubts, often by running around, keeping busy, filling a calendar with meetings, or losing chunks of a day in social media distractions.

*Desist! Be quiet! Know that I am God—and you are not.*

*I will be exalted among the nations.*

*I will be exalted in the earth.*

Calling back to us from the edge of Paradise, that is Good News.

# In God We Trust

"In God I trust. I will not be afraid" (Psalm 56:11).

If you were asked, "Tell me the most familiar phrase in the Bible," you could just take any coin or dollar bill of any denomination and read, "In God We Trust." (Granted, the print on a coin is so small that some of us require a magnifying glass to read it.) The phrase is so commonplace we seldom ponder its biblical roots. Nor do we often consider the circuitous route "in God we trust" traveled to eventually become engraved on our money and named by Congress our official national motto.

It was King David who first coined the phrase, though he was not yet a king when he did so. One thousand years before the birth of Christ and while still a teenager, David defeated the giant Goliath and became the hero of his countrymen, the Israelites. That moment of victory paradoxically launched David on a perilous path. The then-king of Israel, Saul, became extremely jealous of David and in a maniacal, egotistical rage attempted to assassinate the young warrior.

To escape, David fled to a town that, according to some Jewish commentaries, had been commandeered, in a strange twist of fate, by Goliath's brother. After narrowly escaping the wrath of Saul, David found himself once again imperiled by a vengeful enemy. As Goliath's brother and his gang circled, God 'blessed' David with an epileptic fit. Foaming at the mouth, speaking incoherently, contorted in posture, David became convincingly insane. Rather than kill him, the authorities declared him a nuisance and drove him out of town.

The trauma of those narrow escapes from death—at the hands of Goliath, King Saul, and then Goliath's brother—made a profound impression on David, understandably enough. Because David was a song writer as well as a warrior, when he recovered from his episode of insanity, he wrote verses in spiritual ecstasy that may originally have been lyrics to a song and which we know as Psalm 56. "When I am afraid," David sang— and as a battle-tested soldier, he knew fear—"that is when I put my trust in God, whose word I praise. In God I trust without a fear" (Psalm 56:5). Emerging from an existential crisis, David breaks out with "In God I trust" as a triumphant song of praise for God having delivered him from death.

This phrase enters our national lexicon 3,000 years later, in 1814, also at a traumatic moment. We are still an infant nation, again at war with England, and it's clear that we are losing. In August of 1814, the British captured our young capital, Washington, DC, and burned the White House. Then they sent their battleships to bombard Fort McHenry, an American fort which protected nearby Baltimore Harbor.[11] Francis Scott Key, an American lawyer, was at that moment detained on a British war ship in the harbor because he had learned of the imminent attack while negotiating the release of an American citizen. For 25 hours British ships hurled bombs and rockets at Fort McHenry. When the morning dawned and the fog of war lifted, revealing that the British onslaught had failed, Francis Scott Key saw our flag still waving over the fort. Inspired by the sight, he scribbled the poem, *Defense of Fort McHenry*, verses that we now call *The Star-Spangled Banner*.

Francis Scott Key, a devout Episcopalian and amateur poet, had often written on religious themes so it's not surprising that the last verse of *The Star-Spangled Banner* includes the phrase "in God is our trust":

And this be our motto: 'in God is our trust.'

And the star-spangled banner in triumph shall wave

O'er the land of the free and the home of the brave!

Key's poem fit well with the tune of a song popular at the men-only drinking club he frequented. (The popularity of the tune helped it eventually become our national anthem.) The 'motto' lines are a challenging verse actually to sing, however, which may partly explain why we seldom do.

It's also a challenging verse for us to sing today because of what the words meant then. In 1814, this was *not* the land of the free. While America was the home of the brave, it was also the home of the slave, a reality with which Francis Scott Key was intimately familiar. He had served as defense attorney to uphold slavery in court.[12] He himself owned other people—though 15 years after writing *The Star-Spangled Banner* and just prior to his death, he freed his slaves.

The phrase "in God we trust" did not become our national motto during the War of 1812, as Key's poem proposed. It took another half-century before 'in God is our trust' wended its way into our institutional life in a numismatic sense. We trace that journey to a letter from the Rev. M.R. Watkinson, a minister from Ridleyville, Pennsylvania, addressed to the Secretary of the Treasury in November of 1861.[13] Watkinson, knowing that the Secretary of the Treasury was also a Christian, proposed that several biblical words be inscribed on coins:

This would make a beautiful coin, to which no possible citizen could object. This would relieve us from the ignominy [tarnish] of heathenism. This would place us openly under the Divine protection we have personally claimed.[14]

The date of Watkinson's letter is hugely significant: November, 1861. Just seven months earlier, the Confederate States' army had attacked Fort Sumter in South Carolina. That started our Civil War, the bloodiest war in American history, and caused a cultural earthquake whose tremors still rattle us today.

I agree with Rev. Watkinson that using biblical words would make a beautiful coin. I take issue, however, with his assertion that "no possible citizen could object." His belief that printing words on money would "relieve its bearers from heathenism" is questionable theology. But his argument that a biblical phrase "would place us openly under the Divine protection" is a conviction likely held as strongly today in many quarters as it was then.

However, the conviction that certain Americans are under divine protection, suggesting that others are not, is a belief that has its internal contradictions. Rev. Watkinson was writing from his Yankee stronghold in Pennsylvania. The Deep South, fighting to preserve slavery under the Confederacy, was armed with the same Christian Bible and presumably trusted in protection from the same God.

Tensions inherent in biblical interpretation were as pronounced then as they are now. Confederate clergymen certainly knew as well as Rev. Watkinson that the phrase 'in God we trust,' or some close variation of it, appears not only in Psalm 56 but also in ten other psalms: Psalms 9, 22,

34, 40, 91, 118, 121, 143, 145, and 146. Christians from both the North and the South highly valued the Book of Psalms.

There's no evidence that the Secretary of the Treasury weighed the opposing theological nuances and intellectual conflicts that the phrase might stir up. In any event, he did not act on Watkinson's specific recommendation immediately. The Secretary did, however, support the concept. Three years later, with the war dragging on and its outcome yet uncertain, Congress authorized the minting of the two-cent coin with the engraving, 'In God We Trust.'

King David's rapturous shout in Psalm 56, which Francis Scott Key wrote into his *Star-Spangled Banner*, rises up yet again in a time of crisis and lands on other coinage. 'In God We Trust' first appeared only on the two-cent coin, but the phrase gradually appeared on other coins until finally Congress in 1938 determined that *all* United States coins would bear this inscription.

The year of 1938 was also a tumultuous time, as we were deep into the Great Depression and in need of salvation from economic disaster and looming world hostilities. By 1938, 'In God We Trust' was engraved on coins and bills alike, and was embedded in our national consciousness. But it had not yet been named our national motto. That finally came about in 1955 when a Joint Resolution of the 84th Congress declared 'In God We Trust' the national motto of the United States, a Resolution signed into law the following year by President Eisenhower.

The phrase composed by King David had come a long way from the 11 psalms to Francis Scott Key and *The Star Spangled Banner*, to Rev. Watkinson and the two-cent coin during the Civil War, to the requirement that the phrase be inscribed on all our currency. Its journey through time took it through periods of slavery, bloodshed, courage, and patriotism. Its timeline includes emancipation, two world wars, the Great Depression, the beginning of our war on the Korean Peninsula, the struggle with McCarthyism over what it means to be an American, and the start of the Cold War. Finally, 'In God We Trust' became our official national motto in 1955.

The year 1955: Now there's a year that was certainly a major marker in our American culture. It's a year whose events have had long-term impact and that I personally recall with nostalgia.

- Elvis Presley gave a concert in Jacksonville, Florida, which resulted in perhaps the first riot at a rock concert.
- Television aired *The 64,000 Question*, and television game shows have never been the same since.
- ABC started *The Mickey Mouse Club*, proving the popular appeal of fan clubs, even a fan club for a rodent.
- Both Bill Gates of Microsoft and Steve Jobs of Apple were born in 1955. While their contribution to the digital age was 50 years in the future, Ray Kroc started the McDonald's fast food chain that same year, dramatically impacting our American waistline and making his contribution to both convenience and diverticulitis. I have benefitted, and suffered, from the lives of all three men.
- The USS Nautilus launched in January of that year, becoming the first operational nuclear power submarine and altering the global power structures. In November, we sent our first military troops to help train South Vietnamese soldiers in their civil war. This led to an involvement costing 58,220 U.S. military fatalities, including several of my high school and college classmates.[15]
- Emmett Till, a black 14-year-old, was murdered in Mississippi for not showing 'proper' respect to a white woman. Rosa Parks was arrested for refusing to go to the back of the bus. Her arrest precipitated the Montgomery bus boycott, which in turn brought Martin Luther King, Jr., into prominence—and demonstrated that the exercise of global power can't mask internal fissures forever.

As we reflect on the history of the phrase 'In God we trust,' it seems clear there is a consistent desire by many Americans to trust in God and to praise God. But this prompts several questions. Just who is this God in whom we claim to trust? And what should our response be to this God?

Our New Testament asserts that the primary nature of God is love. Throughout the New Testament, Jesus, the Apostles, St. Paul, and the other writers explicitly and concretely show us how we are to respond to a loving God. It means to demonstrate love in our family and practice hospitality to strangers.

Love your neighbor was not a cliché to Jesus.

If God is love, then as Christians should we not interpret the motto 'in God we trust' to mean *in love we trust*? As a follower of Jesus, I want my country to trust God's love by exhibiting that love in ways that challenge many of our current tenets.

- I want a country where a child finds safety in a mother's womb.
- I want a country where a father and mother and their children find safety and shelter at our border, not a border where government officials separate families and relatives.
- I want a country where the person who is too poor to pay for chemotherapy or a knee replacement can still receive full health care—because the fact that Jesus made sick people healthy is recorded in almost every chapter of the Gospels. Shouldn't Christians want to be like Jesus?
- I want a country where no private citizen can own an assault weapon, and where a person who isn't old enough to drive a car can't buy a gun.

I can't speak for pagans or secular people but, as a Christian minister, I want to promote family life and church communities where we are gentle when we could be harsh and where we seek to be agreeable when it's easier to be irritable. As a Christian, I want to trust in a God of love, and act accordingly. I yearn to live in a country where kindness and compassion are not just published in the Book of Psalms and printed on our currency, but also engraved in compassionate policies and charitable behaviors.

# Your Surprise Ending

"Teach us to number our days" (Psalm 90:12).

Psalm 90 is attributed to Moses so it's fair to ask what motivated him to write it and when.

Moses presents robust religious credentials. This special emissary of God had extraordinary encounters with the Almighty on several occasions. There's a tone of familiarity between God and Moses in this psalm, as if we're overhearing an intimate conversation.

Moses starts the conversation at the beginning, both his own and God's. "You have been our dwelling place through all generations" (v.1). He's referring to Israel's history, recalling times when God had provided refuge to Abraham, Isaac, Jacob, and especially Joseph, saving them from extinction. He's also mindful of his own experience when, as an infant, he was rescued out of the bulrushes. The Egyptian pharaoh had decreed that all male Jewish babies should be slaughtered. Providentially, pharaoh's daughter rescues Moses and, with a touch of political irony, he's raised in pharaoh's own household. God has been a "refuge" and a "dwelling place" (the Hebrew can be translated as either metaphor) both to Moses and his people at their most vulnerable moments.

When you are at your most vulnerable, this is a psalm to turn to.

That verb, "turn," is a significant word in this psalm, which in the Hebrew can be translated both as "turn" and "return." It's a word that helps us appreciate a candid debate that Moses is having with God. Moses acknowledges that God has been a dwelling place for all generations. And Moses grants that God exists in a cosmic timeframe. But Moses seems uneasy with the consequences of this relationship. Moses says to God with what we might consider an almost accusatory tone, "You create us, and then You grind us to a pulp. You tell us to turn back to the dust from which we came."

Whoa, hold up there! Is this any way to talk to the King of the Universe? Moses has just acknowledged that God predates creation itself—and then he immediately goes into what amounts to a rather lengthy and heartfelt riff on the unfairness of it all. "We humans are here for only a short time, but we live under your wrath. We look to you for refuge. Then as soon as we show up, we are instead swept away like withered and dry grass, literally tossed into the dust bin of history, all traces of our lives obliterated, erased" (v.5-10).

Moses seems depressed. He erupts poetically in anger and despair, close cousins to depression. Couching his feelings with allusions to the Book of Genesis and its creation stories, Moses confronts God with an issue that still challenges theologians, believers, and sceptics: Why do bad things happen, especially to good people? Not bothering to tiptoe around his conclusion, he blames God's wrath for the human condition.

Moses may also have been feeling a bit guilty when he wrote this psalm. In verse 8 he refers to "secret sins." Moses' most egregious sin is not quite as secret as he had initially hoped. As a young adult, he had been enraged by the injustice of an Egyptian beating a Hebrew slave. Moses killed the Egyptian and buried him in the sand, only to have his murder revealed shortly thereafter. (A sin is not really so secret when it gets recorded in the Bible and we read about it over 3,000 years later.)

Fearing the consequences, Moses ran from the comfortable palace of the pharaoh into the deserts of Midian, living at least 40 years as a desert shepherd. Verse 10 suggests that Moses is nearly 80 years old when he writes this psalm. At this season of his life, with every expectation that the end is near, he's not ecstatic about either his earthly sojourn or that of the human venture.

"Hmmm," we can almost overhear Moses musing to himself, as he realizes what he's just said to God, albeit somewhat lyrically. "Maybe God's wrath has something to do with my behavior. With human behavior." Having acknowledged that God is the Creator, Moses perhaps also accepts that, as the progeny of Adam and Eve, he, too, has been expelled from the Garden of Eden. His life, with or without secret sins, has not been a paragon of godly obedience. Possibly God has every right to be displeased, even angry, with the human condition.

We don't need to inventory our hidden sins or grapple with a changing global climate or rail at political turmoil to realize that we do not inhabit a Garden of Eden. That's self-evident. Often, however, we prefer to deny that our own actions bear some responsibility for unpleasant circumstances.

Many decades ago, I was on a retreat at the Immaculate Heart Hermitage in Big Sur, California. An elderly monk delivered an evening homily on the creation stories in Genesis, observing that we seldom reflect on the consequences of our fallen nature. (John Calvin had, so as a Presbyterian I was predisposed to hear hints of 'original sin.') To summarize the monk's reflections: We live in a fallen world; we behave in ways contrary to the will of a Holy God; we invariably deny our ongoing responsibility in contributing to this fallenness.

For example, I'm reminded of my conversation with a doctor who said that it would be necessary to take out one-quarter of my colon. "I'm not really excited about that option," I replied. "What's my alternative?" "You could have stopped eating so many Big Macs 50 years ago," he replied. (I sensed this was not his first conversation of this sort.)

Smoking causes lung cancer. Speeding can kill. Texting while driving can be harmful to your health. Burning fossil fuels is destroying coral reefs and melting the Alps. Lying politicians threaten our democracy. Denial, in short, doesn't change consequences, a lesson we experience in every facet of life. That we haven't really 'learned' this lesson does not alter inevitable consequences. Many sins are hardly secret. And blaming floods and hurricanes and droughts or wars or cancer or diverticulitis on God's wrath is questionable theology.

If we're living in a fallen world, then the corollary is we live in a world that needs redemption, which was the conclusion of the monk's message. That homily reaffirmed a conviction a high school friend shared with me when we were young men: that while we can't save this world, we can join Jesus in an effort to live a life of some redeeming social value.

I digress from Psalm 90. But so did Moses, even while he was writing it. He found himself tumbling downward in an emotional, spiritual spiral. He wanted to believe that God was a refuge to the people in the past. He hoped God would be a refuge in the future. But he could count. For over

400 years his people had been building pyramids in Egypt. Trapped in poverty and writhing under oppression, they had no prospect whatsoever of entering the land promised to Abraham, Isaac, and Jacob. Moses yearned for a positive end both to the human story and to his own story. "Establish the work of our hands," Moses pleads at the end of his psalm. "Make my life count for something. Let me be remembered, not just deleted" (v.17).

Can we sense Moses' yearning for this tectonic shift in his perspective? Moses first hoists his banner proclaiming this desire in verse 12: "Teach us to number our days, that we might gain a heart of wisdom." I enjoy mathematics. The scriptures give so much attention to numbers, I often think of God as a master mathematician.

But how does counting lead to wisdom?

Maybe it doesn't, at least by itself. Amassing data can lead to intrusion, surveillance, and manipulation, not necessarily to better ways of doing things on behalf of the human venture. Just knowing facts leads to trivial pursuits as well as to medical advances and scientific discoveries. Yet, counting the hours in a day and realizing that "this is the day the Lord has made, rejoice and be glad in it" (Psalm 118:24) certainly have considerable value.

Moses loved numbers, too. By giving us the Ten Commandments and hundreds of rules and regulations in the books of Numbers and Leviticus, it's a short step for Moses to apprehend that gem, "Count your days; gain wisdom" (Psalm 90:12). But it took a miracle for him to unearth this sparkling treasure. If he wrote Psalm 90 at age 80, then he wrote it just before his encounter with the burning bush.

The key word in understanding how Moses went from depression and anger at the start of his psalm, to hope and praise by its conclusion is "turn," the word mentioned previously. "You told us to turn to dust," Moses writes in verse 3. "You turn (return) to us," he says in verse 13. He takes the same Hebrew word used to describe God's wrath and pitches that word right back at God, to call upon God's mercy. We might paraphrase Moses' thought process as follows: "Please don't just turn us to dust. You turn to us and show us pity."

That's a rather hearty if not haughty riposte to thrust into your prayers with the Almighty Ruler of the Universe. While it's not necessarily a gambit I recommend, this psalm does set a precedent for it. The last four verses of the psalm reveal Moses' ultimate requests to God. With a very human mixture of humility and persistence—and, yes, even a bit of audacity—Moses is hopeful that God's compassion will truly be our refuge. He fervently prays that God's love will replace God's wrath, and that our afflictions and our days of trouble will be transformed into days of joy. Rather than consigning us to the Grim Reaper, Moses prays that God will shower humanity with deeds of splendor.

Moses concludes this exceptional conversation with God by placing before God that most universal sentiment of all: "Establish the work of my hands" (v.17). Moses speaks for us all when he begs, "Make my life memorable. Make something that I do endure." Once we've come to the realization that our time is limited, isn't this a fundamental desire? We want to be remembered. That's why we inscribe names on tombstones and place brass plates under stained glass windows and attach our names to companies.

At age 80, Moses had no idea how fully God would answer that prayer. He prays that God will in some fashion erase the pain of the past and replace sorrow with joy. The 40 years in the wilderness did not fully accomplish this, and the Book of Judges shows us that the entrance into the Promised Land did not go exactly the way Moses had anticipated. But the nation of Israel and a Jewish people that has survived more than 3,000 years are testimony to his answered prayer. Moses prayed that his works would last, that something from his hands would be established. Shortly after this prayer, Moses carries the Ten Commandments, first carved in stone and now carved into the foundation of western civilization's legal architecture.

We're not Moses. What we do and accomplish will never be of that magnitude. The audacity with which Moses spoke to God might prove a bit risky to emulate. But we can borrow the intensity of his prayer. The desire to have our lives count for something in the onslaught of randomness and meaninglessness is still pervasive. We want to leave something behind.

We do leave something behind, though most likely it's not what we envision. On my first visit to Israel in 1976, I purchased a small bowl, certified by the Israeli Department of Antiquities as being over 3,000 years old. It's just an ordinary piece of pottery, the type common to every household near the time of Moses. The craftsman who made it may have thought the kids playing next door would break it. There was no thought that this hunk of clay would survive even to the next generation, much less for thousands of years.

Which prompts the question: What have you done that will survive, not in history, but in the mind of God? I guarantee you that it will be a little thing, your little 'pottery dish.' It's something you've forgotten about or even gave no thought to at the time, but that Jesus regarded as highly important. It's the widow's mite, the small coin given at some sacrifice, the cup of water offered to the stranger. It's when you made the coffee and set out doughnuts for the coffee hour after services, or when you handed out the bulletin with a word of greeting, or put the room back in order when everyone had left, and turned out the lights—not because it's a building *per se* but because the church is a place to worship and deserves respect, and the people who come are seeking the Lord and should be honored.

Rich people build big monuments but there's no hint in scripture that God, the architect of the universe, places that much value on our buildings. Even the pyramids are a symbol of oppression, not achievement. God had Jesus born in a cave. None of the chairs or tables Joseph and Jesus built has survived. Jesus predicted that the temple, the pride of King Herod, wouldn't last another half a century. Jesus was buried in a tomb with no marker. Jesus was interested, as was Moses, the man of God, in behavior and in actions, not buildings.

I'm reminded of panning for gold, which one can still do in streams in the Gold Country of California or at tourist mines in Alaska. You take the prospector's pan, gather stones from the river bed, and swish them around in the water. Then you throw out the largest ones because they are worthless rocks. You swish some more, and again throw out the largest. You continue doing this until you get to the very smallest elements. There, hidden until the very end, is the gold.

That's how it was with Moses. You may or may not recall that precisely because of one of the "secret sins" that Moses committed, in an act of disobedience seemingly trivial to us, Moses is not allowed to enter the Promised Land (Numbers 20:10-13). He can only look out from a hilltop in Jordan and see it in the distance. Then he dies. He's counted the days. He's seen wisdom. He left something behind. But he died, ultimately unfulfilled, yearning to experience what he could only see from a distance.

His fulfillment occurred in another dimension altogether. In an account that is mystical in every sense of the word, Jesus meets with Moses on a mountaintop in Israel 1,300 years *after* Moses had died on a mountaintop in Jordan (Matthew 17:3). Finally, Moses has reached the Promised Land. What Moses had prayed for, Jesus fulfilled in a manner that Moses could never have foreseen. Imagine his astonishment.

When Jesus read and prayed Psalm 90, He may have thought to Himself, "I'm going to surprise Moses in a way that he could not possibly have envisioned."

When you and I read and pray this psalm, with finely-tuned spiritual sensitivities, we can perceive the Risen Christ saying, "Will they ever be surprised!"

# It's All in the Family

"As far as the east is from the west,
so far has the Lord removed our transgressions from us" (Psalm 103:12).

Psalm 103 is one of the most memorable, poignant, profound, and prayerful psalms that King David offers us.

David tells us this is an especially consequential psalm by both its structure and its unique vocabulary. Whenever he starts and ends a psalm with exactly the same phrase, which he does only a few times, this is his trademark for saying, "This is special for me." In Psalm 103 he begins, "Bless the Lord, O my soul," and ends with the identical phrase, "Bless the Lord, O my soul." He goes even further. As if typing in a bold font and all capitals, he repeats this exact phrase in the second verse, "Bless the Lord, O my soul, and forget not his benefits." The very structure of the psalm assures us we're walking in the inner sanctum of David's psyche.

He uses special words to further emphasize this point. *Baruch* is the Hebrew word for "blessed." It's the primary word used in the Old Testament to express exceptional honor toward God. *Baruch* embraces a sense of awe and wonder and respect and thankfulness to God. All your Jewish friends know the word *baruch* because they begin many prayers with the phrase, *Baruch atah Adonai*: 'Blessed art Thou, O Lord.'

David also uses the word "soul" to show how intimate this psalm is to him. The word for "soul," which appears over 750 times in the Old Testament, refers to a person's total life-force, total personality, and character. When David begins, "Bless the Lord, O my soul—and all that is within me, bless his Holy Name," he's proclaiming with the full force of language that with every fiber, every muscle, nerve, and brain cell, he blesses and praises the Lord! He repeats the phrase with a burst of energy like a sprinter thrusting out of the starting block.

In virtually every verse, he rehearses the marvelous benefits this loving God provides us: forgiveness of our misdeeds, regeneration of health and energies during our brief sojourn on this globe, and "everlasting and everlasting" love extending into future generations. Then, with an ecstatic crescendo, David envisions an array of angels and the heavenly hosts blessing and praising God. David concludes the psalm euphorically exclaiming for the third time, "Bless the Lord, O my soul!"

The driving question for our reflection on this psalm is: Can you also claim this psalm for yourself?

This psalm is also David's most poignant. With just one verse, he shows us how poignant—painful, really—it is for him to write this psalm. If we were not informed about David's life story, we might easily overlook the verse. But the biblical writers—inspired, many Christians believe, by the Holy Spirit—clearly want us to know David's biography.

The Bible devotes more chapters to David than to any other single person, with the possible exceptions of Moses, Joseph (of the coat of many colors), and Jesus. Yet in comparison to all three of these biblical characters, we know more details of David's youth and adult life than we do about those three men. We know David's childhood occupation and his adolescent exploits. We see the details of the religious, military, and political machinations of his rise to power. We read of his narrow escapes from death and his brutal slaughter of his enemies. We hear the prophetic promises that his progeny will rule for generations.

David also writes some of the most quoted literature in history. We know him as a musician, a songwriter, a poet, and a repentant sinner. We know the details of his rule as a king and how he organized and administered his kingdom. We know his advisors, his chief of staff, and how he commanded his army. And we know the dynamics of his family life. He is the paragon of unrivaled success—in every area except one.

With one phrase David permits us to peek inside his soul and probe that one area: "As a father has compassion on his children" (Psalm 103:13). With this verse David points us back to his own family experience. If we do not understand that one phrase and that family experience, we fail to grasp this psalm.

David's family relationships were, to put it simply, terrible. The Bible paints a picture of David the brother, husband, and father as an extraordinary failure. He's the youngest of eight brothers. The one exchange the Bible records between David and his oldest brother is a fight—a harsh verbal exchange immediately prior to David's fight with Goliath. Instead of having a fist fight with his brother, he goes and kills the giant.

As a husband, David also had some issues. Let's start by observing that he had at least seven wives and ten concubines. A concubine is perhaps similar to what we would call today a mistress. So David had 17 women, all at the same time. Granted, polygamy—having many simultaneous wives—was (and in some instances still is) acceptable in the Middle Eastern culture. But it did present challenges for being a father to children of seven different wives, all sharing the same palace. For David it was a disaster.

The Bible records those disasters and makes no effort to erase or even minimize them. David's oldest son, Amnon, the first in line to succeed him as king, raped and abandoned his half-sister (2 Samuel 13). That young woman, Tamar, the only of David's daughters whom we know by name, was the full sister of Absalom. Absalom comforted his sister while plotting his revenge.

While there is much in this royal family constellation that brought consternation to David, one incident with Absalom especially so branded David's heart like a hot iron that it evoked from him the line in this psalm, "As a father has compassion on his children" (v.13). Absalom may have been David's favorite son. Absalom is the older brother of Solomon, the son who in fact succeeded David and is identified with the Book of Proverbs. Absalom's name is a combination of the Hebrew for father (*abba*) and the word for peace (*shalom*). David obviously felt great affection when he held the infant 'Ab-shalom' in his arms and named him, 'You who bring peace to your father.'

Absalom brought anything but peace. When Absalom learned about his sister's abuse at the hands of their older half-brother, Amnon, Absalom silently harbored revenge for two years. Then he organized a party for all the brothers and sisters, just outside Jerusalem. It was to be a grand celebration.

All the princes and princesses attended this 'royal-kids only' event. As they gathered around the banquet table, Absalom commands his bodyguards, "Go kill my older brother, Amnon." The assassins may have hesitated a bit at first—Amnon was the crown prince, expected to become king someday—but they followed orders. Pandemonium broke out. The other relatives literally ran for the hills while Absalom races for refuge to a neighboring region where the governor happened to be his grandfather.

David, understandably distraught, has lost two sons: his oldest by murder and his favorite by exile. Fast forward several years. Through palace intrigues beyond our immediate interest, David allows Absalom to return to Jerusalem. How does Absalom respond to this act of clemency? Even though he's probably the next in line to become king himself, yet perhaps sensing that during his exile Solomon has undermined his position, Absalom proceeds to foment a revolution against David in order to seize the throne for himself.

There's fine, suspenseful biblical writing around this revolution, but spoiler alert for those of you who may not go read the story yourself: Absalom is successful (2 Samuel 15). Absalom assembles an army and chases David out of Jerusalem. David barely escapes as he runs for his life from his son. Now we're in a brutal civil war. The two sides prepare to confront each other in a dense forest. As David's troops go out to meet the opposing army, David stays behind at the city gates and instructs his soldiers, "Be gentle with my son Absalom."

The father, even when confronted with total rebellion, has compassion for his son.

Absalom's army is defeated. In the rout that ensues, Absalom, crashing headlong through the thickets, becomes stuck in the dense brush, where David's men kill him. They dispatch a messenger to inform King David, who is still waiting at the city gate for news of the battle. "How is my son Absalom?" David anxiously asks the messenger as a father would, but as a soldier he may have anticipated the answer: "All your enemies should be like him" (2 Samuel 18:32).

David's response is the most painful, poignant howl in the entire Bible. "Absalom. Absalom," David sobs. "If only I had died instead of you! O Absalom, my son, my son!" (2 Samuel 18:33).

We're alongside David in the sanctuary of his soul when he writes this psalm. He gives us a transcendent description of God as our loving and forgiving Heavenly Father. As a father pities and has compassion on his children, even the ones who rebel, so the Lord pities us and has compassion on us, even when we turn away from Him.

In David, an earthly father distressed over the friction in his family, we can see our Heavenly Father, sorrowful over frictions in our families and distraught by the hatred that infects the family of nations. As David waited at the gates of the city, yearning for a repentant child, so Jesus waits at the entrance of our souls, hoping we will let Him come into our hearts. With magnificent metaphors, David assures us that God loves us: "As far as the heavens are above the earth, as far as the east is from the west, that's how far the Lord removes our transgressions from us!" (Psalm 103:12).

While the psalm promises that the Lord will love us in spite of our transgressions—just as David continued to love Absalom in spite of Absalom's multiple transgressions—our behavior does carry consequences. Surely Absalom knew the risks while plotting his brother's murder and his subsequent efforts to seize the throne. And surely David knew that his commanders, when they had the opportunity, would slay the enemy they encountered in battle. The power of the psalms, and in particular this one, is that they do not recoil from the complexities of human drama. The love of David the father embraces the son Absalom even while the son engages in rebellious behavior. The father's love cannot save Absalom from the consequences of his actions.

Taken to another level, the unfathomable love of God embraces you even when you engage in immoral or corrupt behavior. The love of God does not void the consequences. However, that love of the Heavenly Father—to use the psalmist's imagery—can heal the wounds.

But perhaps not entirely, in this life. Common sense and lived experience attest that if there is no "next dimension," if there is no heaven or hell, then this world is ultimately unjust. The guilty often go free; the oppressed often die still oppressed; and the innocent often suffer. St. Paul illuminates this reality when he states succinctly in his grand chapter on the resurrection, "If the dead are not raised, 'Let us eat and drink, for tomorrow we die'" (1 Corinthians 15:13).

King David, living 1,000 years before Jesus and the miracle of Easter morning, had intimations throughout his psalms of a heavenly sphere. As inspired as David was, this progenitor of the Messiah heard only whispers of what St. Paul could later claim, "If for this life only we have hoped in

Christ, we are of all people most to be pitied" (1 Corinthians 15:19). But King David did have a vision of a Royal Kingdom when he concludes this psalm with a prayerful paean: "The Lord has established his throne in the heavens, and his kingdom rules over all!" (v.19).

David's conclusion, which is his revelation into how God will manifest God's love to the human condition, prompts me to see his personal, poignant, and profound psalm as also an invitation to pray the psalm. And in keeping with the family context of David's psalm, I want to pay tribute to my mother (of blessed memory) both for her affection for this psalm and for her advice to me on how to pray.

Teaching a child to pray is surely one of the most precious gifts that any parent can give a child. When you pray, my mother taught me, use the words of the Bible. These are the words God gives us, she explained, so these are the words and themes (translated of course from the Hebrew and Greek) that God likes to hear because these are the words the Lord gave us. In her honor, I'll end this chapter by praying as she would if she were using the words of this psalm and interjecting ideas that reflect today's reality.

"Our loving heavenly Father," she would say, "I bless and praise You with all my soul and with all my strength and with all my inmost self. I bless you, Father, for all the good You have shown to me and to my family. Thank You, Lord, for helping me remember all the countless benefits that come to me. You heal the diseases of the body with advances in science and medicine and psychology. You use the intelligence of doctors and nurses and the caring hands of countless people to help me.

"But more importantly, Lord, You heal the diseases of the soul. You have saved me from disasters that I'm not even aware of and from temptations that, without You, would have overpowered me. You don't treat me as my sins deserve. You forgive me. You even gave Your own son Jesus—for me—on the cross. As far as the east is from the west, that's how far You remove my transgressions. And I know that You will redeem my life from the pit and that You will crown me with love and compassion.

"Lord, bless the preachers of Your Word and the congregations that hear Your Word. May we bless You just like the angels who obey Your Word. The angels bless You. May we bless You like the heavenly hosts who do Your will. In heaven they all bless You. And I want to join them!

"Bless the Lord, O my soul! In Jesus' Name, amen."

# Stepping Along

"In distress I cry to the Lord" (Psalm 120:1).

"Where does my help come from?" (Psalm 121:1).

The Psalms of Ascent (Psalms 120-134)

While there is no recognizable order in the sequencing of the 150 psalms, there are several identifiable collections or units of psalms within the Book of Psalms. The 15 psalms numbered 120 to 134 form such a collection. Compiled over a thousand-year span, from the time of King David to the time of Jesus, this ensemble is collectively called the Psalms of Ascents.

The Psalms of Ascents comprise a prayer book within the Book of Psalms and are especially intended to be prayed *en route* to Jerusalem. That geographical destination, Jerusalem, provides the primary reason for their title. Situated in the midst of a mountain range, the city is 2,500 feet above sea level. To reach Jerusalem, you must ascend. You go up, step by step.

That's why this collection of 15 Psalms is sometimes called a Song of Steps. When this collection was translated from the Hebrew into the Greek,[16] its title changed from a Song of Ascents to a Song of Degrees.

All these titles—Psalms of Ascents, Songs of Steps, Songs of Degrees— suggest that reaching God involves a process of spiritual growth. Many steps are required to reach God, which is why each individual psalm is always titled a "Psalm of *Ascents*," in the plural.

Each step is significant but no one step is sufficient.

During the long span over which this prayer book of 15 psalms was written, Jerusalem—whose name has peace, *shalom*, 'Jeru-*shalom*,' at its root—seldom knew peace. Some archaeologists believe it may have been captured and destroyed as many as 20 times through the centuries. Biblical history tells us of the Jews being led out of Jerusalem into the Babylonian captivity, finding no safe harbor along the way. Living in exile especially prompted the writing of the Psalms of Ascents, the desire to climb back up to Jerusalem and to be safe, close to God, in the City of David.

By the time of Jesus, the Jewish people had returned to Israel, although Israel itself was ruled by the Roman Empire. As a religious practice, devout Jewish families traveled to Jerusalem three times a year to celebrate the three pilgrim festivals. How often or how frequently Mary and Joseph made those pilgrimages to Jerusalem with Jesus and his brothers and sisters is a matter of conjecture. Only one occasion is recorded in the Gospels, when Jesus was 12 years old (Luke 2:41-53). Every pilgrimage, however, evoked the recitation of the Psalms of Ascents. Jesus, therefore, knew these 15 psalms from His childhood. The only story we know about Him as a young boy records Him with His family in Jerusalem, having walked there for the Passover (Luke 2:41).

By the time the Holy Family reached Jerusalem, they knew why the Psalms of Ascents had acquired that title. Mary, Joseph, and Jesus began their trip in Nazareth in the region of the Sea of Galilee. They traveled south, following the Jordan River, a 70-mile downhill route known as the Jordan River Rift. The Jordan River empties into the Dead Sea, which is the lowest point on the earth's surface. Just before reaching the Dead Sea, they arrived at Jericho, where the road turns and starts to go up to Jerusalem. Even today, with a modern highway, you experience going up because you ascend 3,700 feet in the 20 miles from Jericho to Jerusalem.

Since going to Jerusalem for Passover was an annual event, Jesus very likely made the trip up that steep mountain trail 15 or 20 times before we meet Him again as a young adult. On each occasion, He's praying the Psalms of Ascents. The Gospels note several times that Jesus is in Jericho and heading toward Jerusalem. Picture Him at the foot of the mountain. Starting the climb, Jesus and His disciples begin praying the Psalms of Ascents.

When you read and sing and pray the Psalms of Ascents, you are sharing the prayers of our Lord.

The 15 psalms of the Psalms of Ascents start at a geographic low point.

They also start from an emotional low point. "In my distress I called out to the Lord" (Psalm 120:1) is the plaintive cry that opens this prayer book. Why this distress? Because the author "dwells in Meshech" and "lives among the tents of Kedar" (v.5).

Meshech is a hostile country to the north of ancient Israel. Meshech reminded the pilgrims of one of those times when Israel had lost a war.[17] Its people had been taken captive, carried off by a barbaric people to Meshech. "I must live among the tents of Kedar," the writer continues. Kedar is a pagan country to the south. Together Meshech and Kedar symbolize Israel's plight. The people are exiled, abandoned. Surrounded by barbarians on all sides, the psalmist in distress calls out to the Lord.

Still today, Jews and Christians in many Middle Eastern countries are persecuted for their faith, forced into exile, and generally ignored by mainline denominations in the United States. Praying the Psalms of Ascents might make us more cognizant of their current plight. And it does not require much religious imagination to think of these psalms as psalms for all refugees and asylum seekers.

They're also personal psalms. Have you ever cried out to God because you were in distress or feeling abandoned or really terrified, just hoping God will answer?

I have.

I was in the emergency room at a hospital in Austin, Texas. I had suffered a stroke. The doctors were trying to determine if I was still in that small window of time when they can administer a very strong drug. If administered within three hours from the onset of the stroke, the prognosis for recovery is high. If, however, the drug is administered outside that timeframe, it can turn the brain to mush. (That's a layman's term.) As the minutes ticked by, the doctors' urgency in probing and testing me increased. My inability to utter a coherent sentence likewise increased. My jumbled brain careened between 'this can't be happening to me' to fearfully sensing that 'something very bad is happening to me.'

Looking into the distraught faces of the doctors, nurses, my wife, and my daughter, I began silently to pray the Lord's Prayer. But I could not get past "Our Father." There were no words. A total blank. I felt distressed— terrified—at what seemed an extremely bleak future. I mean, I could recite the Lord's Prayer before I knew how to spell my own name. Now I couldn't remember more than two words!? Then I realized that even though I could not *say* the words of the Lord's Prayer, I could *feel the rhythm* of the Lord's Prayer. I could sense the cadence of the prayer that I had experienced so many times in worship: "Our Father//Who art in heaven//hallowed be Thy Name..."

I was not praying the Lord's Prayer. The Lord's Prayer was praying me.

In the midst of our distress, where do we go to get help? That's exactly the question the psalmist asks in the next prayer in the Psalms of Ascents prayer book: "I lift up my eyes unto the hills. Where does my help come from?" (Psalms 121:1). He answers his own question. "My help comes from the Lord," *not* from the hills.

He's not referring to nature and the forests in the hills. The "hills" are where the Canaanites live who worshipped Baal and their pantheon of gods.[18] Baal was the Canaanite storm god, sometimes pictured riding on the clouds, holding a thunderbolt, and swinging a mace. The hills were filled with pagan enemies who worshipped idols and practiced lewd sexual behavior.

When the psalmist looked into the hills, he's seeing the battlefield between Baal and Yahweh, the God of Abraham, Isaac, and Jacob. He's seeing himself surrounded by a culture seething with evil. He instinctively and passionately cries out, "*My* help comes from the Lord, the Maker and Creator of heaven and earth" (v.2).

As the people of God, we are surrounded just as the psalmist was centuries ago. We feel distress. We fight fierce battles, both cultural and theological. Fortunately, we have the prayer book of Jesus: the Book of Psalms which includes the Psalms of Ascents. As you study and reflect on the psalms, let me draw upon my own experience and suggest that you seek the Lord, step by step:

Read the psalms.

Sing the psalms.

Pray the psalms.

When you need them the most, the psalms will pray you.

# Search and Destroy!

"Search me and know my heart" (Psalm 139:23).

Since King David wrote Psalm 139 a thousand years before the birth of Christ, David obviously didn't have a Baptist hymnbook which included the song, *Just a Little Talk with Jesus*. David didn't know Jesus. But David did know God, and David knew how to have a little talk with God.

In this psalm, David bares his soul with candor and honesty. By its genuine expression of emotions, Psalm 139 illuminates the ways we can share our personal feelings with our Lord. What a gift to us that the Holy Spirit has recorded David's intimate "just a little talk with God" and preserved it through the centuries for our benefit!

The key word, "search," both begins and concludes the psalm: "O Lord, you have searched me" (v.1) and "Please search me" (v.23). From the beginning of his life and through all his adventures, David realizes God has searched him. In the final verses, David pleads with God to continue searching him in order to lead him into the future, the "way everlasting." David is not describing a one-and-done moment with God, but a lifetime of scrutiny.

Meditating upon this psalm is not for the spiritually faint of heart. Is this psalm for you? Are your willing to be searched by God?

This is not a Google search where information is scanned, surveyed, and selected. The Hebrew word translated as "search" is a military term. It means being watched and tested in battle. The commander searches—watches, tests—the soldiers to see if they are reliable and trustworthy for confronting the enemy. David, who has been a soldier and the commander of an army, realizes that God is testing him and, by extension, every one of us on the battlefield of life.

Let's admit it: God's search is not always entirely comfortable. Verse 4 reads, "Before a word is on my tongue, You know it completely, O Lord." Fortunately, most of the time we're praising God and saying polite, even nice things, about other people. But perhaps there are moments when we've said something unkind or less than flattering about someone else. We think they're just words on our tongue.

However, our vocabulary certainly got Jesus' attention, for He said, "By your words you will be justified and by your words we will be condemned" (Matthew 12:37). James, the brother of Jesus, refers to the tongue's power to praise *and* poison throughout his brief letter (The Letter of James). Today, James would post on his social media page that Twitter was an extension of the tongue.

Generally our words are positive and intentional but, other times, they just escape like little demons from a self we thought we had conquered.

In the spirit of the psalms, I'll interrupt my commentary with an embarrassing confession. My wife, Gail, and I were on a bike ride on the canal path between Washington's Crossing and New Hope, Pennsylvania. There had been a heavy rain the day before that made the path muddy and slippery. I had negotiated several dozen sloppy spots, feeling rather proud of my expertise, when at literally the last mud puddle I lost control of the bike and fell. I landed on my left knee, the same knee that had recently undergone surgery for a total knee replacement. My wife helped pry the bike off me—she had been just behind me and watched this whole event as if it were in slow motion. We slowly pedaled the seven miles back to our car and called the doctor's office. The doctors assured me their metal knee replacement was fine—they were very proud of their work—and that my soft tissue around their replacement would feel better in a few weeks.

The next day, with the kind of timing unique to a spouse, Gail asked me after my morning devotions if I knew what I had said as I was falling. Well, of course I remembered. With the entire English dictionary to choose from, and quite familiar with those words of praise we offer every Sunday, I yelled words that reflected my years as a student at a men's college. Those were not the words I would want on my lips when I make my transition from here to the Promised Land!

"From the same mouth come blessing and cursing" (James 3.10). God heard what I said. God didn't have to search my heart and mind very hard to know my vocabulary. I didn't have to go to the heights of heaven or the depths of Hades or the far ends of the earth to realize that I can't escape God's hearing. All I had to do was fall off a bicycle a few miles from home.

In Psalm 139, David poetically surveys the contours of his life with all its different terrains and in all its tumultuous circumstances. He's sharing with us his little talk with God and saying, "I'm sorry about a lot of things, Lord God Almighty, but I still want to praise you and I know you continually care for me."

David knows that God has searched him and tested him, and yet continues to be with him and to hear him.

Just as David realizes that God hears everything, David also realizes there is no place where we can evade God's gaze.

God's gaze starts at our creation. David didn't know about ultrasound when he proclaims, "When I was woven together…Your eyes, O God, saw my unformed body" (v.15). God puts our bodily parts together as one weaves cloth or makes a basket.[19] "You knit me together in my mother's womb" (v.13), he writes. The Hebrew word translated "knit together" is also translated, "You have *covered* me in my mother's womb." And when this Hebrew word is a noun, it can refer to a protective shield for the troops that storm a city wall (Nahum 2:5).[20]

In the protection of the womb, shielded from the forces of culture that await at birth and under God's watchful eye, the limbs of the child come together in secret. David articulates poetically what you know scientifically: how your first vertebrae are laid down, your spinal canal formed, the foundation for your brain and nervous system established, and the rudiments of your eyes appear—all when in your mother's womb you are about the size of a poppy seed[21] or an aspirin tablet!

God is everywhere. God knows everything. You likely agree with this and could comment on this central theological statement if this were an adult education class. Here I'll merely note that even if we *say* that God knows everything and is everywhere, we often *act* as if God is not paying attention to us.

To use a very homey illustration. Years ago when we were first married, my wife and I had a puppy, a wonderful German Shepherd. The dog was usually well-behaved but, being a puppy, it sometimes failed to display proper adult dog behavior. One act of puppy disobedience would occur when we left it alone for several hours. It would chew on our plants, splattering leaves and dirt and pottery. Upon our return, I would try to shame it ('You naughty dog, you'). The dog would merely turn its head away. This puppy, otherwise a reasonably intelligent creature, seemed to believe that if *he* could not see me, *I* could not see him.

Isn't that sometimes the way we feel about God? If we just ignore God on certain occasions, God will ignore us. Not so, insists the psalmist.

The darkness is as light to You.

How precious, O Lord, are Your thoughts.

When I awake, I am still with You! (v.12).

Apparently, David awakens with a nightmare in verses 19 through 22. Suddenly he interrupts this gently flowing, majestic poem with scathing words: "If only you would slay the wicked! Do I not hate those who hate you? I have nothing but hatred for them!"

I don't like the fact that my biblical hero David would be this candid in his violent outburst. I'm predisposed to defend him. But I do not need to defend King David. He's one of the most significant men in history. We know more about his family background, his early career, his life as a warrior, poet, and statesman than nearly any other person in the Bible. He's identified with more Old Testament biblical literature than any other writer, with the possible exception of Moses. His psalms permeate the New Testament and were on the lips of Jesus at the cross. Clearly, biblical writers and the Holy Spirit hold David in singularly high regard. King David hardly needs me to defend him in his passionate paroxysm against those who defy God.

That said, I will make a few observations on his behalf as we consider verses so troubling that they are frequently ignored. In my Presbyterian hymnbook, for instance, this entire psalm is printed—except for these few angry verses. The hymnbook editors are implying that the verses would cause biblical indigestion for the average Presbyterian. Best to leave them out. Then I checked a Baptist hymnbook. Guess what? That hymnbook also printed Psalm 139 minus these same verses. The Baptist editors apparently thought they would give Baptists spiritual indigestion. Those hymnbook editors left out verses the Bible puts in. No one would notice.

Well, we just noticed.

Read carefully, however, and realize that David is not asking for revenge against those who are his personal enemies. From his teenage years when he fought Goliath, to his days as king, to his declining old age, he had foiled countless would-be assassins—even friends and family members. But he's not asking for vengeance against them. Nor is he asking permission to slay the wicked himself. He is asking that God handle the situation: "If only You would slay the wicked, O God."

Even so, in whatever way you decide to look at it, these verses which are deleted from hymnbooks yet recorded in the Bible are breathtaking in their admission of "perfect hatred" toward those who hate and maliciously defy God.

How un-Jesus like.

That is, until we recall some of the things that Jesus said. Then these anger-filled verses, in their hatred of evil and their call for God's judgment on wickedness, seem to anticipate words of Jesus that are so harsh our hymnbook editors might want to prune them from the New Testament. To quote Jesus:

This is how it will be at the end of the age. The angels will come and separate the wicked from the righteous, and throw the wicked into the fiery furnace, where there will be weeping and grinding of teeth (Matthew 13:49).

These are harsh words from Jesus, yet they are not too distant from those of his famous ancestor King David, who predated him by 28 generations and 1,000 years.

Rather than ignore these verses, I will—admittedly with some trepidation—tread where the editors of the hymnbook did not, and confront these passages. I can imagine that someday, in Heaven's Promised Land, I will be attending a Bible study class that King David is conducting. In that distant dimension, I want to ask him, "What was the circumstance that prompted your passionate not-politically-correct emotional explosion? Who were the wicked people who defied God? And how did you achieve such an intense desire to serve God that you could 'hate those who hated God?'"

In this imaginary, futuristic Bible study class, I actually don't think David will answer my question satisfactorily. (I mean, apart from, who am I to ask King David anything?!) I envision him instead turning to me and saying that the circumstances which prompted his outburst were unique to him. Instead of telling me what motivated his outburst on behalf of a righteous God, he's likely to ask *me* some searching questions about my threshold for anger.

Let's turn the volume up a notch. Let's suppose that in that heavenly Bible study, sitting alongside King David, we also see the prophets Isaiah, Jeremiah, Amos, Micah, and countless martyrs and human rights activists. What if they say, "We want to have a little talk with Gregg!" They will want to know what, if anything, prompted my outrage against evil and my passion on behalf of the Gospel during my life time. "Don't you love justice?" they might ask. "Aren't you concerned about mercy? Aren't you outraged when people around you defy God?"

Frankly, there is much today that kindles my fiery outrage as a minister of Jesus of Nazareth. We are living in a period of American history when compassion for the most vulnerable among us has been replaced with cruelty. We have powerful policy makers who for many years have been nearly maniacal in their efforts to make health care inaccessible and unaffordable to millions of Americans. If there is any one activity that best describes the behavior of Jesus, it is that of His healing everyone who asked Him.

Why would any follower of Jesus want to make access to health care difficult and expensive?

Think also of the Dreamers. Their parents brought them here as infants, often escaping atrocities, and they have grown to adulthood with the dream of becoming citizens. They probably grew up thinking they *were* citizens. The rest of us likely thought so, too, since they look and act like any young Americans with hopes and dreams. We know the importance of young people having dreams. Discriminatory policies masking unwarranted prejudices create the nightmare of deportation.

President Trump used the powers and prejudices of a former senator from Alabama to justify kidnapping children at our border. Their zero-tolerance policy is a vicious zero-compassion policy. It expresses the concept of segregation in hateful dimensions. Their administration carries out this depraved practice with consequences that will damage children into the third and fourth generation. This administration's actions replicate some of the vilest behavior in America's past, and their shame will live in infamy for all of America's history. Do I not hate such policies that are infected by the virus of injustice? I find them disgusting, indefensible, and thoroughly unChristian.

The racial component to what President Trump says and does displays a repugnant mindset that must be challenged. As Dr. Martin Luther King, Jr., preached, "There comes a time when silence is betrayal."[22] While racial animosities run rampant through his presidency, his policies, and his Cabinet, our silence is a betrayal of our country's highest values and our Christian faith's deepest principles.

I think David might have gone a little too far when he expressed his hatred toward God's enemies, though I don't expect to have the courage to tell him that to his face. I don't hate *people* who are encased in their prejudices and swaddled in their stereotypes. At least, I try not to hate them. First of all, there are too many of them. A CBS News poll found that 83% of Republicans approve of President Trump's handling of racial issues.[23]

Besides, I also know too many of them and I know them too well. I grew up with them. I went to college with them. I drank with them, I danced with them, and I dated them. And I really try not to hate the policy makers who scarcely hide their prejudices. I do hate their policies, however, and I grieve that they are so distant from any teaching of Jesus that I can recognize.

But more than what I hate is what I love. I hate President Trump's wall because I love the cross of Christ. Jesus in His life and at His cross yearns to bring us together in unity. Everything about the cross contradicts everything that President Trump and his minions say about the wall. Because of our love for the cross of Jesus, we should be saying, with the passion of David and in the spirit of Martin Luther King, Jr., that we hate, we despise the evils that try to divide us.

After David's outburst, there was a long poignant pause. Then he prayed from the core of his soul, "Search me, Lord, and see if there is any wicked or evil or unjust way in me" (v.23-24). David was having his little talk with God, and he realized that he was being tested.

To paraphrase Dr. King, there is an urgency to this moment in our American history. Based on my talk with Jesus, I believe that we are being tested—as a country, as a culture, as followers of Christ. Perhaps Psalm 139 can help us in this testing time.

Surely the God who knit us together in our mother's womb, before we knew that skin had a color, wants to knit us together in human community, all our colors in harmony with each other.

Surely the Creator God who weaves our separate cells into hearts and lungs and arms and legs is the same protective Heavenly Father who is painfully concerned for all His suffering children.

Speaking both as a minister and as an American citizen, I am convinced that God is searching and testing pagans and Christians alike.

God does not care if America is great.

God does care—Jesus Christ cares—that America is merciful and just.

# Between the Pasture
# and the Palace

"David escaped to the cave of Adullam" (Psalm 142).

David is in a chase scene, running for his life, finding momentary refuge in a cave in the region of Adullam. This remote area in the hills just to the west of Bethlehem was sparsely inhabited during Old Testament times. Not much beside a few archaeological ruins exist there today. Go to Google Images and search for the phrase "Cave of Adullam" to find many pictures that will help you visualize the terrain in which David, as a refugee, found himself.

Shortly after he's discovered at the Cave of Adullam, David retreats even further into the wilderness area of Israel and finds shelter in yet another cave. Out of those cave experiences, he writes Psalm 57 and Psalm 142.

You are already familiar with many highlights of David's life, but unless you've recently read 1 Samuel 16 through 22, a brief flashback will help place his cave experiences in context.

We are in Israel approximately 1,000 years before the birth of Christ. Saul had been installed as the first king of Israel but, because of his greed, self-centeredness, and spiritual disobedience, God decided to replace him. God selected a one-person calling committee, the prophet Samuel, to find Saul's successor. God gave Samuel some specific but not totally precise instructions: "Go to the house of Jesse of Bethlehem. I have chosen one of his sons for you to anoint as king." God also gave Samuel one important caveat: "Do not consider his appearance or his height," God said to Samuel, "for the Lord does not look at the things that man looks at. Man looks at the outward appearance [I might add, so do women] but the Lord looks at the heart" (1 Samuel 16:7).

Perhaps the prophet Samuel thought, "This shouldn't be too difficult. How many sons can Jesse have?" It turns out, Jesse had eight. So Samuel has Jesse bring his sons forward one by one for their job interview. Apparently they were all seemingly well qualified. But as Samuel met each of the first seven sons and seemed about to make a choice, the Lord stopped him every time. Finally, Samuel said to Jesse, "I've seen seven sons. Great. But don't you have any more?" "Just the youngest," Jesse replied. "His name is David, but he's out in the pasture, taking care of the sheep."

Freeze frame your mental picture here for a moment. David, the youngest son, who became one of the most significant leaders in all of world history, had been relegated to the lowliest position in the family hierarchy. He's out in the pasture, so lightly regarded by his own parents that he's not even invited into the house to meet this special guest!

Have you ever felt rejected or looked down on by anyone in your family? What about having the sense that people ignore you? Maybe your boss or manager or board does not recognize your contributions, and even friends fail to appreciate your real worth. It's easy to feel left out, and in hospitals or nursing homes, to feel humiliated. *You* might think you are qualified for a better position and certainly deserve more respect—but, like David, sometimes you don't even get invited to the party. Getting to a palace appears impossible.

Here's a life-lesson for us in the story of David: Do not confuse where you are with where you ought to be.[24]

Stated in spiritual terms: Do not confuse where you *are* with where God *destines* you to be. The "pasture" you are in is not necessarily the "palace" for which you are intended.

Samuel anoints David with oil, the symbol for David to become king, and now all his older brothers cheer, "Atta boy! Good job! You're the boss and we salute you!" Not quite. The brothers send David back to the pasture and they go off to war.

You know this part of David's biography. He takes lunch to his brothers at the battlefield, ends up slaying Goliath, gets elevated to a high command by King Saul, is given Saul's daughter in marriage—and thereby arrives at the royal palace. Seemingly as the prophet Samuel had predicted, David has gone from the pasture to the palace and is in line to become king.

The problem is that it's the wrong palace. Just as David could not wear Saul's armor when he went to fight Goliath, David cannot inhabit Saul's palace. It's not the palace for which he's been anointed, however appealing it may appear. David himself almost mistook his quick success for his true destination. Jealousies and palace politics showed him otherwise. Saul decides to kill David.

Which brings us to the cave psalm. David, running for his life from the government of Saul, arrives at the Cave of Adullam. Soon afterwards he's joined by his family and 400 men.

Sometimes I hear people say, "God has a sense of humor." Maybe so, but in these verses it looks like a cruel joke. Take off any rose-tinted Bible glasses and look at the people who now surround David. His brothers and his father—they're the very people who ignored him and mocked him and gave him the worst family chores. But since they are David's relatives, and since Saul is trying to kill David, clearly Saul has threatened the entire family. They are not too pleased about forfeiting their property and having to flee to David, who's hiding out in a cave. "Look what a mess you have gotten us into now!" we can hear them saying, along with many versions of "I knew you would never amount to anything!"

David's now stuck in this cave with very cranky family members. Look at the other people God soon sent his way. "All those who were in distress or in debt or discontented gathered around him" (1 Samuel 22:2). The word had gone out. If you're depressed, go hook up with this guy David. If you're poor, if you're on food stamps, if you can't afford housing, if you suffer from mental illness, or if you're just an all-around malcontent, go join David the refugee in his cave.

I've seen a lot of job postings but I've never read one that said, "If you're really unhappy and fretful, apply here." I know a lot of ministers and I've visited a lot of churches, but I've never seen an invitation to a new membership class that read, "We're looking for the poor and depressed and disabled."

It's safe to say, there in the cave, David and those disgruntled folks were not psychologically or spiritually where God intended them to be. And the "cave" you are in is not the "palace" God has in store for you.

We Christians reflect on the psalms and on the life of David because we find in this literature much that anticipates the life of Christ. Notice the people who were drawn to Jesus, whom the Gospels describe in virtually every chapter: the blind and crippled, the hungry, and those imprisoned and in need of health care. While the people drawn to Jesus were not in a literal cave, they were cast out, abandoned, hurting.

In Psalm 142, David describes the cave-like emotional experience of being cast down, literally meaning bent over. David's job was to lead the people with him in that space to a better place. People who come to Jesus are often bent over in mind, spirit, and body. In His strength, we can reach a better place. "Come to Me," Jesus offers, "all you who are weary and carry the weight of many burdens, and I will give you rest" (Matthew 11:28). When we come to Jesus, let's not confuse where we are with where He will lead us.

One afternoon, I and a few others were invited to visit a man who was literally on his death bed. He was under hospice care, lying in a small darkened bedroom of his son's house. This gentleman—I'll call him Pops, since it was the only name I knew him by as we briefly greeted each other in church over the past several years—was comatose. Nine of us gathered around Pop's bed—six adults and three 12-year-old kids—holding each other's hands. Each one of us was also touching him, while the church deacon gave a beautiful, heartfelt prayer.

Pops was in a cave. But Pops was headed to a heavenly palace. A few days later, Pops joined the saints in the Commonwealth of Heaven.

Don't confuse your current predicament with your ultimate destination.

As I have pondered the description of the people who gathered around David at the cave and try to picture them—those in distress and in debt and discontented—the phrase that comes to my mind may also have occurred to you: "Give me your tired, your poor, your huddled masses yearning to breathe free." Listen to the rest of that sonnet which many of us identify with our Statue of Liberty:[25]

"Keep, ancient lands, your storied pomp!" cries she
With silent lips. "Give me your tired, your poor,
Your huddled masses yearning to breathe free—
The wretched refuse of your teeming shore.

Send these—the homeless, tempest-tossed—to me:
I lift my lamp beside the golden door!"

Our government has tarnished this inscription by our inhumane and depraved immigration policies and practices. To separate children from their parents who arrive as refugees or asylum seekers at our border just because they are homeless and tempest-tossed (and not Caucasian), does not speak well for us as Americans. "If you do it to the least of these, you do it to Me," said Jesus (Matthew 25:40). We are not treating Jesus very kindly, which does not speak well for us as Christians.

Like many Christians, and like many Americans, I do not want to confuse where we are now as a nation with who we are meant to be.

David from his cave cried out to God for help. He probably wanted very well-educated officials who could help him administer a kingdom and highly-skilled engineers who could help him build a country. He was certainly not looking for brothers who mocked him, political refugees running from King Saul, and unskilled laborers who could only work the fields.

Here's another take-away lesson from the text.

When we need assistance, God does not always send us the people we expect. God does, however, expect us to work with the people He sends.

That's exactly what David did. If you read a little further in the story, you see where he settles his parents, too old and frail to travel with him, in a safe location. He begins to develop his leadership and administrative skills. Read even further in the story and you'll find that, after several decades, the assortment of folks who gathered around David has grown from that motley band of 400 into an army 800,000-strong in the northern part of his kingdom with an additional 500,000 warriors in the southern part.

David moved from the humility of the pasture through the humiliation of the cave to the prestige of the palace.

The people with him had grown as well, and not just in numbers. David concludes Psalm 142 with the phrase, "The righteous will surround me!" (v.8). They become transformed from masses huddled at the entrance of the cave to righteous citizens of the kingdom.

St. Paul carries this theme of future righteousness to an exalted level when he writes:

What the eye has not seen, nor the ear heard, or the mind of man conceived, *That* is what God has prepared, for those who love Him (1 Corinthians 2:9).

We should not confuse the members of our contemporary Christian organizations with those people who will share celestial glory with us. The Promised Land will also include the very migrants, refugees, abused women, and wounded children whom we currently exclude from this land.

To return to the quotation at the Statue of Liberty: It's not *on* the statue itself. Emma Lazarus wrote the words as a fundraiser for the *pedestal* of the statue. The fundraiser was a success and the platform for the Statue of Liberty was built—but the poem itself was forgotten until several years after she died. Friends of hers then began a campaign to memorialize the poem, as a result of which it's now on a plaque mounted inside the pedestal.

A similar moment of amnesia regarding the noble ideas enshrined in this poem afflicts both our policy makers and large portions of the Body of Christ. Rather than have those words mounted inside the pedestal, they need to be embedded in our hearts.

When there is a revival of Lady Liberty's ideals and an awakening of Christian values, then as Americans and as Christians we will become transformed into the righteous people Jesus Christ wants us to be.

# Deeper Disciples

"I am Thy servant" (Psalm 143:12).

Why study the Book of Psalms? It's an interesting question. One answer is because the psalms comprise the prayer book of Jesus. Jesus quotes the psalms directly or indirectly throughout his ministry. Verses of three of the psalms are on the lips of our Lord when He was on the cross: "My God, my God, why have you forsaken me?" from Psalm 22; "Into Thy hands I commit my spirit," from Psalm 31, and "I thirst," an allusion to Psalm 69:21. There are references in the New Testament to approximately 120 out of the 150 psalms. In the entire Psalter there are 2,450 verses. Nearly 500 of these verses, or 20 percent of the total, are directly reflected in the New Testament. The theology of the psalms can rightly be said to comprise the framework for the theology of the New Testament, alongside the books of Isaiah and Deuteronomy.[26]

Stated another way, if we are to understand the mind of the Master, and if we hope to pray with the power of Christ Himself, then we do well to study and meditate upon the same prayer book which He used, the Book of Psalms.

One of the first things to do when studying any biblical passage is to place it in its historical context. Few texts relate only to their historical period, but often it helps to lift the curtain and see the passage displayed on the stage of its own contemporary scene.

The psalms themselves assist us in finding the context by providing a phrase, almost a title, for each psalm. Some translations do not always include these titles, and other translations abbreviate or slightly modify them. The RSV translation of Psalm 143, for example, is entitled, "A Psalm of David, the prayer of a soul in distress."

The Book of Psalms gives credit to at least eight different authors. It's helpful to know when a psalm is attributed to King David (more than 70, total) because the Bible records so many stories about him that we can try to align the dynamics of a Davidic psalm with particular episodes in his life.

Over the centuries, rabbis and ministers have identified Psalm 143 with two different events in David's life. One is when his son Absalom revolted against him, an especially calamitous time. The other incident is when King Saul chases David in a jealous rage, trying to kill him. This second context makes a bit more sense to me, at least in part because it closely aligns with the dynamics of the preceding psalm.

The chase scene extends over several rather exciting chapters. David and his small band of men are trapped in a cave. Hearing the army at the entrance, they crawl in pitch blackness, deeper and deeper, until they reach its uttermost depths. *We* know the end of the story—that David will survive this near-catastrophe and emerge as one of the greatest figures in human history. But David didn't know how his life story would end. David only knew that he was hunted, trapped, helpless. As a young man in his mid-twenties, he was certain he was about to die.

As we sense David's distress, the words of the psalm now strike us as quite compelling:

Hear my prayer, O Lord.

The enemy has pursued me, crushed me,

and made me sit in *darkness* like those long dead (Psalm 143:1-3).

The Hebrew word "darkness" is actually in the plural form, "darknesses." It could be translated, "darkness within darkness."

Have you ever felt so alone, or so frightened, or in such despair, that it seemed like "darkness within darkness" to you? If so, then you can appreciate David's dilemma and sense that this psalm addresses you.

What does one do when enveloped in "darkness within darkness"? Verses 5 and 6 provide us with David's answer. First of all, he keeps his focus—on God. He recalls the nature of God. Notice the verbs: He remembers, he meditates, he muses—on God. The temptation and even our natural inclination are to meditate on whatever our bleak situation might be. Another popular approach is to deny the situation and claim a positive attitude. "When you're really feeling depressed," I heard a popular television preacher say, "just smile." There's nothing wrong with smiling, I suppose, but David's response, not surprisingly, is more profound. He turns to a study of the nature of God and finds his refuge in the Almighty.

Intermingled with this focus on God is David's desire for *more* of God. "Like a beggar," he says, "I stretch out my hands to you. And like parched land waiting for even a dew drop, my soul thirsts for you" (Psalm 143:6).

When you confront challenges in your life, this psalm—like many of the psalms—suggests a beneficial response. Find your focus in God our Creator, whom we find revealed in Christ, and desire a closer, deeper, increasingly personal relationship with Him.

How do we develop a closer relationship with God in Christ? A primary answer is invariably "through prayer." We can use the psalms—the prayer book of Jesus—to assist us.

One specific way is to use the words of the psalm itself as our prayer. It's what you might call a prayer of the breath.[27] Find a word or a phrase that speaks to you in the psalm (any psalm, though I'm using Psalm 143 as our example here) and incorporate those words into your breathing pattern.

For example, verse 10 contains several brief word combinations:

Teach me to do Thy will, for Thou art my God.

Take the phrase "teach me." When you breathe in, silently say the word "teach," and when you breathe out, the word "me." Repeat. Teach….me, teach…me, teach…me.

You might also use the phrase "Thy will," breathing in on "Thy" and out on "will": Thy…will, Thy…will, Thy…will. (Or, for people not raised on the King James Version of the Bible, Your…will, Your…will, Your…will.) You don't need to be in any special place or mood to practice a prayer of the breath. It's a useful practice for any repetitive action like lifting weights at the gym, pedaling a bike, washing dishes, walking up or down steps, watching the turn signal blink on the car in front of you, waiting in line, or waiting on hold.

Another way to incorporate psalms into your spiritual journey and make the Lord's prayer book your prayer book requires more effort and imagination than just breathing. The following approach is helpful when you have been asked to pray for another person and you are willing to spend some time in prayer. I call it a dynamic, or interactive, reading of the psalms.[28]

This dynamic way of prayer turns the psalm (again, any psalm, not just Psalm 143) from a first-person prayer to a third-person prayer by inserting the name or pronoun for the person who is on your heart.

Here's an example. A colleague sent me an email saying that she had just been diagnosed with breast cancer, asking me to pray for her. We all frequently get requests (or make requests) for prayer. It's a beautiful way of sharing the fabric of our lives and the lives of those in our congregation with each other. Praying for a person, using the spiritual fiber of the psalms in a dynamic fashion, helps.

If you turn to Psalm 143, you can better see what I'm doing. Beginning the prayer at verse 7, let us pray:

> In her darkness within darkness, O Lord Jesus, make haste to answer her and to comfort her, for her spirit—generally so confident and buoyant—fails. Do not hide Your face and Your loving kindness from her.

> Let her hear in the morning—and continually throughout the day—of Your steadfast love. For in You, and in Your healing powers, and in the healing ambassadors You have sent to her, she places her trust.

> Deliver her, Lord Jesus, from this cancer and from all things malignant which threaten her soul and body.

> Teach her the way she should go and extend Your wisdom into the wisdom of her doctors and nurses, for she has turned to You for refuge.

> Let Your good spirit lead her on a level path.
> Preserve her life, Lord, and bring her out of trouble, for Your Name's sake. For she is Your servant. She is Your servant, Lord Jesus. I am Your servant, Lord Jesus.

> The people gathered around her in prayer are Your servants, Lord Jesus. Please hear our requests, for we pray in the strong and certain name of Jesus Christ our Lord.

Why study the Book of Psalms? Personally, I search the psalms because I'm looking for Jesus, whose Holy Spirit infuses them. Sometimes, in some verses, I sense Him clearly. Other times, less so. The Quaker writer Thomas Kelly, though not directly referring to the psalms, expresses a similar desire in *A Testament of Devotion*.[29]

> There is a way of life so hid with Christ in God that in the midst of the day's business one is inwardly lifting brief prayers, subdued whispers of adoration and of tender love to the Beyond that is within. No one need know about it. I only speak to you because it is a sacred trust, not mine but to be given to others. One can live in a well-nigh continuous state of unworded prayer. There is no hurry about it all. It is a life unspeakable and full of glory, an inner world of splendor within which we, unworthy, may live. Some of you know it and live in it. Others of you may wistfully long for it. It can be yours.

I believe that the Book of Psalms reveals the inner life of Jesus. It's not a secret: We can find Him there.

# Endnotes

1   A.B. Simpson, *The Holy Spirit*, vol. 1 (Harrisburg, PA: Christian Publications, Inc., n.d.), 135.

2   David W. Torrance and Thomas F. Torrance, ed., *Calvin's New Testament Commentaries: The Gospel According to St. John*, part 2, trans. T.H.L. Parker (Grand Rapids, MI: Wm. B. Eerdmans Publishing Company, 1979), 120.

3   Rabbi Avrohom Chaim Feuer, *Tehillim/Psalms: A New Translation* (Brooklyn, NY: Mesorah Publications, Ltd., 2013), 61.

4   Peggy Noonan, "Declarations," *Wall Street Journal* (January 31-February 1, 2015): A13.

5   Phillip Keller, *A Shepherd Looks at the 23rd Psalm* (Grand Rapids, MI: Zondervan, 1970). Although I grew up playing on farms in Indiana, I'm relying upon Keller's experience regarding sheep described in this excellent book.

6   Feuer, *Tehillim/Psalms*, 405.

7   Feuer, *Tehillim/Psalms*, 406.

8   Leonard Cohen, "Anthem," *The Future* (November 1992), https://www.leonardcohenfiles.com/album10.html#78.

9   Anne Sexton, "Letter Written on a Ferry While Crossing Long Island Sound," https://www.poemhunter.com/poem/letter-written-on-a-ferry-while-crossing-long-island-sound/.

10  "Who Were The Sons of Korah in the Old Testament?" *Got Questions*, https://www.gotquestions.org/sons-of-Korah.html.

11  I highly recommend a visit to Fort McHenry, a National Monument and Historic Shrine in Baltimore, Md.

12  "Francis Scott Key," *Wikipedia*, https://en.wikipedia.org/wiki/Francis_Scott_Key.

13  Billy Hallowell, "Here's the Deep History Behind 'In God We Trust,'" *Deseret News: Faith* (August 1, 2016), https://www.deseretnews.com/article/865659185/Heres-the-deep-history-behind-In-God-We-Trust.html.

14  U.S. Department of the Treasury, "History of 'In God We Trust,'" *About: Education* (March 8, 2011), https://www.treasury.gov/about/education/Pages/in-god-we-trust.aspx.

15  "Vietnam War U.S. Military Fatal Casualty Statistics: Electronic Records Reference Report," *National Archives: Military Records* (April 29, 2008), https://www.archives.gov/research/military/vietnam-war/casualty-statistics.

16  *The Septuagint Version of The Old Testament and Apocrypha* (Grand Rapids, MI: Zondervan, 1977), 775.

17  Feuer, *Tehillim/Psalms*, 1507.

18  Bruce M. Metzger and Michael D. Coogan, eds., *The Oxford Companion To The Bible* (Oxford: Oxford University Press, 1993), 70, 825; Pat Alexander, ed., "Nations and Peoples of the Bible," *The Lion Encyclopedia of the Bible* (Tring, England: Lion Publishing, 1986), 286.

19  "5526. cakak," Strong's: Hebrew, *Bible Hub*, http://biblehub.com/hebrew/5526.htm.

20  Ibid.

21  Cleveland Clinic, "Fetal Development: Stages of Growth,", https://my.clevelandclinic.org/health/articles/7247-fetal-development-stages-of-growth.

22  Martin Luther King, Jr., "Beyond Vietnam" (sermon delivered April 4, 1967, New York), The Martin Luther King, Jr. Research and Education Institute, Stanford University https://kinginstitute.stanford.edu/king-papers/documents/beyond-vietnam.

23  Steven W. Thrasher, "Why Do You Need the N-word Tape?" *New York Times* (August 19, 2018), https://www.nytimes.com/2018/08/17/opinion/sunday/n-word-tape-trump-racism-omarosa.html.

24  I am grateful to Pastor Anthony C. Talton, Mt. Olivet Baptist Church, Haddonfield, NJ, for this insight.

25  Emma Lazarus, "The New Colossus," *Selected Poems and Other Writings* (2002), https://www.poetryfoundation.org/poems/46550/the-new-colossus.

26  Henry M. Shires, *Finding The Old Testament In The New* (Philadelphia: Westminster Press, 1974), 126-130; 145.

27  This type of silent prayer can be traced to the Desert Fathers of the 4th century. For example, see *The Philokalia*, vol. 1, compiled by St. Nikodimos and St. Makarios (London & Boston: Faber and Faber, 1979). I first experienced this style of prayer in the 1970's at the Iona Center in Redwoods, CA, under Marv Hiles, director, and began applying it to the Book of Psalms.

28  I have no memory of when I first began praying like this, but I'm sure I learned it from someone and did not arrive at it on my own.

29  Thomas R. Kelly, *A Testament of Devotion* (New York: Harper & Brothers, 1941), 122.

# Discussion Questions

**An Invitation**

- What leads you to this book?
- How would you describe your prayer life currently? In what ways might you want to strengthen it?
- If you are studying this book as part of a group, why have you come today? There may be answers that you are not comfortable sharing. If there is information which you do feel comfortable sharing, it may forge helpful points of connection with others in your group.

**Your Battlefield Promise**, Psalm 1

- When your life feels like a battle, which biblical words bring you strength? How do they mesh, or clash, with the words of Psalm 1?
- The psalm moves from conflict to triumph, from violent clashes to a kind of peaceful resolution. Where do you see your life on this spectrum?
- If you have a regular practice of meditating on the Bible, what is it and how did that develop? How do you believe it serves you?
- If you do not yet have a regular practice of meditating on the Bible, what has hindered you?
- Have you ever felt transplanted from a less nourishing environment to a place that you could thrive, like a tree by streams of water (Psalm 1:3)? What happened? What changed for you? What role do you think prayer played in this change?

**From Despair to Exaltation,** Psalm 22

- Psalm 22 vividly depicts a desperate situation, with bulls and dogs closing in, laughter and scorn on all sides. As you reread the psalm, which images stand out for you and why?
- Most people have experienced at least a few periods of hopelessness in their life. What would—or does—give you strength to move past feeling hopeless?
- What particular words are helpful for you? What do you focus on?

**Your Best Protection,** Psalm 23

- Psalm 23 contains some of the most quoted verses in all of scripture. What is your strongest memory involving this psalm?
- After reading this chapter, what new ideas or understandings surfaced for you?
- Sometimes we can confuse what we need and what we want. How do you make this distinction for yourself?
- When you feel yourself straying like a lost sheep, how do you get yourself closer to green pastures?
- What other ways occur to you to use this psalm now, to live it now, to apply it now?

**The Best Experience Yet,** Psalm 34

- The commentary on this psalm warns that even small lies can get people into trouble. In what kinds of situations would you have considered it acceptable to lie?
- Under what circumstances do you find it easy to praise God?
- When is it hard for you to praise God? What strategies does the commentary suggest that might help you in those circumstances?

**The Peaceable Kingdom,** Psalm 37

- As the commentary observes, almost half of the verses of Psalm 37 promise variations of utter ruin for the wicked. Why do you suppose the psalmist found this message important enough to repeat so many times?
- Attending church, admiring the natural world, and caring for the needy are suggested as ways to take delight in the Lord. In what ways do you take delight in the Lord?
- How do you personally do good on behalf of others? How does your church do good in the world?


**Seeking Good News,** Psalm 46

- The commentary places Psalm 46 in context and suggests that to believe some of its verses ("God makes wars cease to the ends of the earth," for example) may be naive. Discuss how you feel about this.
- More generally, what do you do with passages in the Bible that are difficult to believe?
- In the single verse in Psalm 46 that is attributed to God, the commentary suggests that "Be quiet" can either be an invitation to meditation or an imperative for humility. Which translation speaks more clearly to you and why? How can you apply this verse in your life?


**In God We Trust,** Psalm 56

- The commentary begins by asking about the most familiar phrase from the Bible, "In God we trust." What are your associations with this phrase?
- How would you make the case *in favor of* having the words "In God We Trust" appear on U.S. currency? How would you make the case *against* having those words—or any words from the Bible—appear on our currency or serve as the motto for the United States?

- What difference does it make that there are many different religions that use the word, "God," not just the Judeo-Christian tradition we have in the psalms?
- The commentary describes David composing at least portions of this psalm after an unlikely escape made with God's help. Where do you feel God and/or Jesus Christ is working in your life now? What positive experiences have you had for which you directly credit God?

## Your Surprise Ending, Psalm 90

- Psalm 90 invites us to think about what we have done in our lives that may outlast us. What are three things you have done that you would like to survive as "monuments"? What are two more things you would like to add to the list while there is still time?
- Have you ever made a practice of "numbering your days," perhaps using a calendar or journal? What are the advantages and disadvantages of such a practice?
- What small thing have you observed someone do or have done yourself that had disproportionately larger consequences for good?

## It's All in the Family, Psalm 103

- The commentary clarifies the biblical understanding of "soul" as one's total life-force, including personality and character. How does this definition of "soul" square with your own?
- Which verses reinforce the idea that this psalm may have been written at a moment of personal anguish?
- How do we love those in our life—children, parents, those in our care—when their behavior distances them from us emotionally or physically?
- If you've ever received instruction or advice about how to pray, what was it? How has that instruction or advice influenced your life?

**Stepping Along,** Psalms 120 to 134

- In the midst of your distress, where do you go to get help?
- Have you ever undertaken a pilgrimage, like Jewish families did by traveling to Jerusalem? What inspired you to do so? What are your strongest memories of that experience?
- How does your new understanding of the Songs of Ascents relate to your feelings about immigration and asylum seekers?
- The commentary offers a personal anecdote of feeling a prayer intensely, of feeling like one is *being prayed* as opposed to praying. If you relate to such an experience, what was the circumstance?


**Search and Destroy!** Psalm 139

- The psalmist's petition for God to "search" him means God is watching and testing. To what extent are you willing to be searched by God?
- What do you learn about yourself when you sense that God is searching you?
- The commentary discusses the danger our words can get us into sometimes, escaping "like little demons from a self we thought we had conquered." What practice do you have for helping yourself mind what you say? If, as so often happens, you were too late to stop the words, what do you do then?
- The commentary offers several strong judgments about some of President Trump's policies, no doubt offending or challenging many readers of a different persuasion. How do faith and politics intersect for you? Do you try to hold them in separate spheres in your life, or do you believe that faith and politics are necessarily linked? Does your faith inform your politics, or do your politics inform your faith?

**Between the Pasture and the Palace,** Psalm 142

- The commentary sheds some light on the dynamics of David's nuclear family. How does this information affect the meaning of Psalm 142 for you?
- The psalmist seems hopeful that the place he is in is not what God intends for him. Have you ever had the sense that God has a different place in store for you? How would you describe your "pasture" or "cave" and your "palace"? How did you—or how would you—go from pasture to palace?
- The commentary on this psalm includes the idea that God does not always send us the people we expect. When have you had a sense that someone in your life was sent to you by God?

**Deeper Disciples,** Psalm 143

- As the commentary notes, Psalm 143 points to some of David's strategies for focusing on what matters in a time of "darkness within darkness." How could you use David's strategies in your own times of great distress?
- Which words from this psalm or any other psalm would you select for your own breath prayer (one or two words for inhalation and one or two for exhalation)? In what situations could you see yourself using your breath prayer?
- What are one or two new ways that you envision incorporating the psalms, Jesus' prayer book, into your life going forward?

# Selected Psalms: 1, 22, 23, 34, 37, 46, 56, 90, 103, 120-121:2, 139, 142, 143

## Psalm 1

1. Happy are they who have not walked in the counsel of the wicked,
   nor lingered in the way of sinners,
   nor sat in the seats of the scornful.

2. Their delight is in the law of the Lord,
   and they meditate on his law day and night.

3. They are like trees planted by streams of water, bearing fruit in due season,
   with leaves that do not wither.
   Everything they do shall prosper.

4. It is not so with the wicked.
   They are like chaff, which the wind blows away.

5. Therefore the wicked shall not stand upright when judgment comes,
   nor the sinner in the council of the righteous.

6. For the Lord knows the way of the righteous,
   but the way of the wicked is doomed.

Psalm 22

For the director of music. To the tune of *The Doe of the Morning*.
A psalm of David.

1. My God, my God, why have you forsaken me?
   Why are you so far from saving me,
   so far from my cries of groaning?

2. My God, I cry out by day, but you do not answer,
   by night, but I find no rest.

3. Yet you are enthroned as the Holy One;
   you are the one Israel praises.

4. In you our ancestors put their trust;
   they trusted and you delivered them.

5. To you they cried out and were saved;
   in you they trusted and were not put to shame.

6. But I am a worm and not a man,
   scorned by everyone, despised by the people.

7. All who see me mock me;
   they hurl insults, shaking their heads.

8. "He trusts in the Lord," they say,
   "let the Lord rescue him.
   Let him deliver him,
   since he delights in him."

9. Yet you brought me out of the womb;
   you made me trust in you, even at my mother's breast.

10. From birth I was cast on you;
    from my mother's womb you have been my God.

11. Do not be far from me,
    for trouble is near
    and there is no one to help.

12. Many bulls surround me;
    strong bulls of Bashan encircle me.

13. Roaring lions that tear their prey
    open their mouths wide against me.

14. I am poured out like water,
    and all my bones are out of joint.
    My heart has turned to wax;
    it has melted within me.

15. My mouth is dried up like a potsherd,
    and my tongue sticks to the roof of my mouth;
    you lay me in the dust of death.

16. Dogs surround me,
    a pack of villains encircles me;
    they pierce my hands and my feet.

17. All my bones are on display;
    people stare and gloat over me.

18. They divide my clothes among them
    and cast lots for my garment.

19. But you, Lord, do not be far from me.
    You are my strength; come quickly to help me.

20. Deliver me from the sword,
    my precious life from the power of the dogs.

21. Rescue me from the mouth of the lions;
    save me from the horns of the wild oxen.

22. I will declare your name to my people;
    in the assembly I will praise you.

23. You who fear the Lord, praise him!
    All you descendants of Jacob, honor him!
    Revere him, all you descendants of Israel!

24. For he has not despised or scorned
    the suffering of the afflicted one;
    he has not hidden his face from him
    but has listened to his cry for help.

25. From you comes the theme of my praise in the great assembly;
    before those who fear you I will fulfill my vows.

26. The poor will eat and be satisfied;
    those who seek the Lord will praise him—
    may your hearts live forever!

27. All the ends of the earth
    will remember and turn to the Lord,
    and all the families of the nations
    will bow down before him,

28. for dominion belongs to the Lord
    and he rules over the nations.

29. All the rich of the earth will feast and worship;
    all who go down to the dust will kneel before him—
    those who cannot keep themselves alive.

30. Posterity will serve him;
    future generations will be told about the Lord.

31. They will proclaim his righteousness,
    declaring to a people yet unborn:
    He has done it!

## Psalm 23
### A psalm of David.

1. The Lord is my shepherd, I shall not want.

2. He makes me lie down in green pastures
   and leads me beside still waters.

3. He restores my soul.
   He leads me in paths of righteousness, for his name's sake.

4. Even though I walk through the valley of the shadow of death,
   I will fear no evil, for you are with me.
   Your rod and your staff comfort me.

5. You prepare a table before me, in the presence of my enemies.
   You anoint my head with oil. My cup overflows.

6. Surely goodness and mercy will follow me all the days of my life,
   and I will dwell in the house of the Lord forever.

Psalm 34
Of David.
When he pretended to be insane before Abimelek,
who drove him away, and he left.

1.  I will extol the Lord at all times;
    his praise will always be on my lips.

2.  I will glory in the Lord;
    let the afflicted hear and rejoice.

3.  Glorify the Lord with me;
    let us exalt his name together.

4.  I sought the Lord, and he answered me;
    he delivered me from all my fears.

5.  Those who look to him are radiant;
    their faces are never covered with shame.

6.  This poor man called, and the Lord heard him;
    he saved him out of all his troubles.

7.  The angel of the Lord encamps around those who fear him,
    and he delivers them.

8.  Taste and see that the Lord is good;
    blessed is the one who takes refuge in him.

9.  Fear the Lord, you his holy people,
    for those who fear him lack nothing.

10. The lions may grow weak and hungry,
    but those who seek the Lord lack no good thing.

11. Come, my children, listen to me;
    I will teach you the fear of the Lord.

12. Whoever of you loves life
    and desires to see many good days,

13. keep your tongue from evil
    and your lips from telling lies.

14. Turn from evil and do good;
    seek peace and pursue it.

15. The eyes of the Lord are on the righteous,
    and his ears are attentive to their cry;

16. but the face of the Lord is against those who do evil,
    to blot out their name from the earth.

17. The righteous cry out, and the Lord hears them;
    he delivers them from all their troubles.

18. The Lord is close to the brokenhearted
    and saves those who are crushed in spirit.

19. The righteous person may have many troubles,
    but the Lord delivers him from them all;

20. he protects all his bones,
    not one of them will be broken.

21. Evil will slay the wicked;
    the foes of the righteous will be condemned.

22. The Lord will rescue his servants;
    no one who takes refuge in him will be condemned.

# Psalm 37
## Of David.

1. Do not fret because of those who are evil
   or be envious of those who do wrong;

2. for like the grass they will soon wither,
   like green plants they will soon die away.

3. Trust in the Lord and do good;
   dwell in the land and enjoy safe pasture.

4. Take delight in the Lord,
   and he will give you the desires of your heart.

5. Commit your way to the Lord;
   trust in him and this is what he will do:

6. He will make your righteousness shine like the dawn,
   your vindication like the noonday sun.

7. Be still before the Lord
   and wait patiently for him;
   do not fret when people succeed in their ways
   when they carry out their wicked schemes.

8. Refrain from anger and turn from wrath;
   do not fret—it leads only to evil.

9. For those who are evil will be destroyed,
   but those who hope in the Lord will inherit the land.

10. A little while, and the wicked will be no more;
    though you look for them, they will not be found.

11. But the meek will inherit the land
    and enjoy great peace.

12. The wicked plot against the righteous
    and gnash their teeth at them;

13. but the Lord laughs at the wicked,
    for he knows their day is coming.

14. The wicked draw the sword
    and bend the bow to bring down the poor and needy,
    to slay those whose ways are upright.

15. But their swords will pierce their own hearts,
    and their bows will be broken.

16. Better the little that the righteous have
    than the wealth of many wicked;

17. for the power of the wicked will be broken,
    but the Lord upholds the righteous.

18. The blameless spend their days under the Lord's care,
    and their inheritance will endure forever.

19. In times of disaster they will not wither;
    in days of famine they will enjoy plenty.

20. But the wicked will perish:
    Though the Lord's enemies will be like the flowers of the field—
    they will be consumed, they will go up in smoke.

21. The wicked borrow and do not repay,
    but the righteous give generously.

22. Those the Lord blesses will inherit the land,
    but those he curses will be destroyed.

23. The Lord makes firm the steps
    of those who delight in him.

24. Though you may stumble, you will not fall,
    for the Lord will upholds you.

25. I was young and now I am old,
    yet I have never seen the righteous forsaken
    or their children begging bread.

26. They are always generous and lend freely.
    Their children will be a blessing.

27. Therefore, turn from evil and do good.
    Then you will dwell in the land forever.

28. For the Lord loves the just
    and will not forsake his faithful ones.
    Wrong doers will be completely destroyed
    and the offspring of the wicked will perish.

29. The righteous will inherit the land
    and dwell in it forever.

30. The mouths of the righteous utter wisdom,
    and their tongues speak what is just.

31. The law of their God is in their hearts;
    their feet do not slip.

32. The wicked lie in wait for the righteous,
    intent on putting them to death;

33. but the Lord will not leave them in the power of the wicked
    or let them be condemned when brought to trial.

34. Hope in the Lord
    and keep his way.
    He will exalt you to inherit the land;
    when the wicked are destroyed, you will see it.

35. I have seen a wicked and ruthless man
flourishing like a luxuriant native tree,

36. but he soon passed away and was no more.
Though I looked for him, he could not be found.

37. Consider the blameless, observe the upright;
a future awaits those who seek peace.

38. But all sinners will be destroyed;
there will be no future for the wicked.

39. The salvation of the righteous comes from the Lord;
he is their stronghold in time of trouble.

40. The Lord helps them and delivers them;
he delivers them from the wicked and saves them,
because they take refuge in him.

Psalm 46
For the director of music.
Of the Sons of Korah.
A song.

1. God is our refuge and strength,
   an ever-present help in trouble.

2. Therefore we will not fear, though the earth give way
   and the mountains fall into the heart of the sea,

3. though its waters roar and foam
   and the mountains quake with their surging.

4. There is a river whose streams make glad the city of God,
   the holy place where the Most High dwells.

5. God is within her, she will not fall;
   God will help her at break of day.

6. Nations are in uproar, kingdoms fall;
   he lifts his voice, the earth melts.

7. The Lord Almighty is with us;
   the God of Jacob is our fortress.

8. Come and see what the Lord has done,
   the desolations he has brought on the earth.

9. He makes wars cease
   to the ends of the earth.
   He breaks the bow and shatters the spear;
   he burns the shields with fire.

10. He says, "Be still, and know that I am God;
    I will be exalted among the nations,
    I will be exalted in the earth."

11. The Lord Almighty is with us;
    the God of Jacob is our fortress.

Psalm 56
For the director of music.
To the tune of "A Dove on Distant Oaks."
Of David.
A miktam.

1.  Be merciful to me, my God,
    for my enemies are in hot pursuit;
    all day long they press their attack.

2.  My adversaries pursue me all day long;
    in their pride many are attacking me.

3.  When I am afraid, I put my trust in you.

4.  In God, whose word I praise—
    in God I trust and am not afraid.
    What can mere mortals do to me?

5.  All day long they twist my words;
    all their schemes are for my ruin.

6.  They conspire, they lurk,
    they watch my steps,
    hoping to take my life.

7.  Because of their wickedness do not let them escape;
    in your anger, God, bring the nations down.

8.  Record my misery;
    list my tears on your scroll—
    are they not in your record?

9.  Then my enemies will turn back
    when I call for help.
    By this I will know that God is for me.

10. In God, whose word I praise,
    in the Lord, whose word I praise—

11. in God I trust. I will not be afraid.
    What can man do to me?

12. I am under vows to you, my God;
    I will present my thank offerings to you.

13. For you have delivered me from death
    and my feet from stumbling,
    that I may walk before God
    in the light of life.

Psalm 90
A prayer of Moses the man of God.

1. Lord, you have been our dwelling place
   throughout all generations.

2. Before the mountains were born
   or you brought forth the whole world,
   from everlasting to everlasting you are God.

3. You turn people back to dust,
   saying, "Return to dust, you mortals."

4. A thousand years in your sight
   are like a day that has just gone by,
   or like a watch in the night.

5. Yet you sweep people away in the sleep of death—
   they are like the new grass of the morning:

6. In the morning it springs up new,
   but by evening it is dry and withered.

7. We are consumed by your anger
   and terrified by your indignation.

8. You have set our iniquities before you,
   our secret sins in the light of your presence.

9. All our days pass away under your wrath;
   we finish our years with a moan.

10. Our days may come to seventy years,
    or eighty, if our strength endures;
    yet the best of them are but trouble and sorrow,
    for they quickly pass, and we fly away.

11. If only we knew the power of your anger!
    Your wrath is as great as the fear that is your due.

12. Teach us to number our days,
    that we may gain a heart of wisdom.

13. Relent, Lord! How long will it be?
    Have compassion on your servants.

14. Satisfy us in the morning with your unfailing love,
    that we may sing for joy and be glad all our days.

15. Make us glad for as many days as you have afflicted us,
    for as many years as we have seen trouble.

16. May your deeds be shown to your servants,
    your splendor to their children.

17. May the favor of the Lord our God rest on us;
    stablish the work of our hands for us—
    yes, establish the work of our hands.

Psalm 103
Of David.

1. Praise the Lord, my soul;
   all my inmost being, praise his holy name.

2. Praise the Lord, my soul,
   and forget not all his benefits—

3. who forgives all your sins
   and heals all your diseases,

4. who redeems your life from the pit
   and crowns you with love and compassion,

5. who satisfies your desires with good things
   so that your youth is renewed like the eagle's.

6. The Lord works righteousness
   and justice for all the oppressed.

7. He made known his ways to Moses,
   his deeds to the people of Israel:

8. The Lord is compassionate and gracious,
   slow to anger, abounding in love.

9. He will not always accuse,
   nor will he harbor his anger forever;

10. he does not treat us as our sins deserve
    or repay us according to our iniquities.

11. For as high as the heavens are above the earth,
    so great is his love for those who fear him;

12. as far as the east is from the west,
    so far has he removed our transgressions from us.

13. As a father has compassion on his children,
    so the Lord has compassion on those who fear him;

14. for he knows how we are formed,
    he remembers that we are dust.

15. The life of mortals is like grass,
    they flourish like a flower of the field;

16. the wind blows over it and it is gone,
    and its place remembers it no more.

17. But from everlasting to everlasting
    the Lord's love is with those who fear him,
    and his righteousness with their children's children—

18. with those who keep his covenant
    and remember to obey his precepts.

19. The Lord has established his throne in heaven,
    and his kingdom rules over all.

20. Praise the Lord, you his angels,
    you mighty ones who do his bidding,
    who obey his word.

21. Praise the Lord, all his heavenly hosts,
    you his servants who do his will.

22. Praise the Lord, all his works
    everywhere in his dominion.
    Praise the Lord, my soul.

# Psalms 120
## A song of ascents.

1. I call on the Lord in my distress,
   and he answers me.

2. Save me, Lord,
   from lying lips
   and from deceitful tongues.

3. What will he do to you,
   and what more besides,
   you deceitful tongue?

4. He will punish you with a warrior's sharp arrows,
   with burning coals of the broom bush.

5. Woe to me that I dwell in Meshek,
   that I live among the tents of Kedar!

6. Too long have I lived
   among those who hate peace.

7. I am for peace;
   but when I speak, they are for war.

Psalms 121.1-2
A song of ascents.

1. I lift up my eyes to the hills—
   where does my help come from?

2. My help comes from the Lord,
   the Maker of heaven and earth.

## Psalm 139
### For the director of music. Of David. A psalm.

1. You have searched me, Lord,
   and you know me.

2. You know when I sit and when I rise;
   you perceive my thoughts from afar.

3. You discern my going out and my lying down;
   you are familiar with all my ways.

4. Before a word is on my tongue
   you, Lord, know it completely.

5. You hem me in behind and before,
   and you lay your hand upon me.

6. Such knowledge is too wonderful for me,
   too lofty for me to attain.

7. Where can I go from your Spirit?
   Where can I flee from your presence?

8. If I go up to the heavens, you are there;
   if I make my bed in the depths, you are there.

9. If I rise on the wings of the dawn,
   if I settle on the far side of the sea,

10. even there your hand will guide me,
    your right hand will hold me fast.

11. If I say, "Surely the darkness will hide me
    and the light become night around me,"

12. even the darkness will not be dark to you;
    the night will shine like the day,
    for darkness is as light to you.

13. For you created my inmost being;
    you knit me together in my mother's womb.

14. I praise you because I am fearfully and wonderfully made;
    your works are wonderful,
    I know that full well.

15. My frame was not hidden from you
    when I was made in the secret place,
    when I was woven together in the depths of the earth.

16. Your eyes saw my unformed body;
    all the days ordained for me were written in your book
    before one of them came to be.

17. How precious to me are your thoughts, God!
    How vast is the sum of them!

18. Were I to count them,
    they would outnumber the grains of sand—
    when I awake, I am still with you.

19. If only you, God, would slay the wicked!
    Away from me, you who are bloodthirsty!

20. They speak of you with evil intent;
    your adversaries misuse your name.

21. Do I not hate those who hate you, Lord,
    and abhor those who are in rebellion against you?

22. I have nothing but hatred for them;
    I count them my enemies.

23. Search me, God, and know my heart;
    test me and know my anxious thoughts.

24. See if there is any offensive way in me,
    and lead me in the way everlasting.

Psalm 142
A *maskil* of David.
When he was in the cave.
A prayer.

1. I cry aloud to the Lord;
   I lift up my voice to the Lord for mercy.

2. I pour out before him my complaint;
   before him I tell my trouble.

3. When my spirit grows faint within me,
   it is you who watch over my way.
   In the path where I walk
   people have hidden a snare for me.

4. Look and see, there is no one at my right hand;
   no one is concerned for me.
   I have no refuge;
   no one cares for my life.

5. I cry to you, Lord;
   I say, "You are my refuge,
   my portion in the land of the living."

6. Listen to my cry,
   for I am in desperate need;
   rescue me from those who pursue me,
   for they are too strong for me.

7. Set me free from my prison,
   that I may praise your name.
   Then the righteous will gather about me
   because of your goodness to me.

# Psalm 143
## A psalm of David.

1. Lord, hear my prayer,
   listen to my cry for mercy;
   in your faithfulness and righteousness
   come to my relief.

2. Do not bring your servant into judgment,
   for no one living is righteous before you.

3. The enemy pursues me,
   he crushes me to the ground;
   he makes me dwell in the darkness
   like those long dead.

4. So my spirit grows faint within me;
   my heart within me is dismayed.

5. remember the days of long ago;
   I meditate on all your works
   and consider what your hands have done.

6. I spread out my hands to you;
   I thirst for you like a parched land.

7. Answer me quickly, Lord;
   my spirit fails.
   Do not hide your face from me
   or I will be like those who go down to the pit.

8. Let the morning bring me word of your unfailing love,
   for I have put my trust in you.
   Show me the way I should go,
   for to you I entrust my life.

9. Rescue me from my enemies, Lord,
   for I hide myself in you.

10. Teach me to do your will,
    for you are my God;
    may your good Spirit
    lead me on level ground.

11. For your name's sake, Lord, preserve my life;
    in your righteousness, bring me out of trouble.

12. In your unfailing love, silence my enemies;
    destroy all my foes,
    for I am your servant.

# About the Author

Award-winning producer J.W. Gregg Meister earned his BA from Williams College and MDiv from Princeton Theological Seminary, and his MA in Radio and Television from San Francisco State University and MA in Communications from the Annenberg School for Communication at the University of Pennsylvania. He founded Interlink Media in 1988 (interlinkmedia.net). He and his wife, Gail, currently live in New Jersey.

Printed in the United States
By Bookmasters